The Leadership Edge

The Leadership Edge

Think, Behave, and Communicate Like a Leader

Michael B. Ross and Mike Shaw

BEP

BUSINESS EXPERT PRESS

Leader in applied, concise business books

The Leadership Edge: Think, Behave, and Communicate Like a Leader

Copyright © Business Expert Press, LLC, 2025

Cover design by Cindy Beebe Langley

Interior design by Exeter Premedia Services Private Ltd., Chennai, India

First published in 2024 by
Business Expert Press, LLC
222 East 46th Street, New York, NY 10017
www.businessexpertpress.com

ISBN-13: 978-1-63742-720-0 (paperback)
ISBN-13: 978-1-63742-721-7 (e-book)

Business Expert Press Human Resource Management and Organizational Behavior Collection

First edition: 2024

10 9 8 7 6 5 4 3 2 1

Description

Businesses rise, fall, or stall based on their level of leadership. Businesses that invest the time, energy, and resources to develop leaders enjoy a competitive edge—and by developing leaders who can develop other leaders, unleash the power of rapid and sustainable growth. By developing people with the skills to put team members and customers in the best position to succeed, they ensure their own success.

The Leadership Edge gives business leaders and leadership coaches, consultants, and trainers a framework for developing strong business leaders who can learn to develop other strong business leaders. It serves as a guide, offering insights, strategies, and practical tools to empower individuals and organizations to gain their own leadership edge.

Whether you are a seasoned executive, a middle manager, an emerging leader, or a leadership consultant, the principles and practices explored in *The Leadership Edge* provide the knowledge and resources to unleash your leadership potential and make a meaningful impact on your organization.

Contents

Introducing Michael Ross

Michael Ross has been speaking about leadership and teaching leadership skills since 2008. He has logged over 10,000 hours of training, coaching, and consulting business owners, executive leaders, mid-level managers, and entrepreneurs on how to think, behave, and communicate like leaders. He has founded, owned, and operated four successful businesses: all but one he started from scratch, twice without any investment capital; all he built to be profitable and sustainable; one he sold at six times his total investment. Along the way, he earned two advanced degrees and multiple certifications in leadership and management.

"But more valuable than the successes," Ross insists, "are my failures. Two businesses I founded, owned, and operated didn't make it. I started them, tried to build them, fell short, and eventually had to shut them down. I've spent a lot of money on products, services, methods, and programs that didn't work."

Ross also readily admits to leadership failures.

"I've over-promised and under-delivered. I've been unclear in my vision, goals, and expectations. I've had great intentions but poor execution. I've lost my temper and treated people poorly. I've made bad decisions that hurt people. My failures have resulted in broken relationships."

Ross can describe in detail how painful each of those failures was, but he will also tell you that he wouldn't have the success he enjoys these days without them.

"I learned so much from those experiences. Each time I failed I made a conscious choice to get back up, even when I felt unworthy and unsure. Because I didn't give up, I was able to improve, to amend my errors in judgment in business and leadership. Now I'm making better decisions and living with fewer regrets."

Today, as Principal of High Performance, a business of HBK, a Top 50 accounting firm with more than 700 professionals across seven service lines, Ross leads a team of consultants helping businesses and entrepreneurs improve organizational performance through personal skills development and education. He and his team are making real, bot-tom-line differences for companies, enabling their leaders with real, sub-stantive leadership skills that translate into real, measurable contributions in terms of profitability and sustainability.

When it comes to business leadership, Ross has the experience, exper-tise, successes, and scars to speak meaningfully and convincingly. In *The Leadership Edge*, he shares the insights he has gained over the years from his personal successes and failures as well as from his body of work with businesses large and small, developing effective, productive leaders.

Foreword

In a world of unprecedented speed of change and innovation, I welcome you to a catalyst for transformational leadership. In this book, Michael crafts threads of wisdom and experience. This book serves as both a compass and a mirror for those who aspire to lead others or those who seek to become the best version of themselves—a personal view into the highest levels of leadership.

To me, leadership, in its truest form, is part art and science, a delicate balance between guiding and empowering, vision and execution, and self and the collective team. It is a journey that requires courage, resilience, and an unwavering commitment to personal growth. Through the pages that follow, you will encounter thoughts and lessons on how leaders can navigate through the many challenges of leading others and the blessings that come as well.

My foreword serves as an invitation—a call to embark on a personal journey. A journey that will not only highlight the principles and practices of effective leadership but will also challenge you to reflect on your own capacity to inspire, to motivate, and to effect change. Each chapter is crafted with the intent to offer insights and strategies that are both timeless and adaptable, principles that can be woven into your own individual journey.

As you turn these pages, allow yourself to be curious and explore the multifaceted nature of leadership. Let the stories, lessons, and reflections found herein help fuel and ignite your personal passion for leading others. Michael understands and highlights that the pursuit of power is not leadership, but rather a commitment to service, innovation, and the collective good.

In an era of fast-paced change that cries out for visionary leaders, this book is an inspired guide for those who care to make a difference in the world through the calling of leading and inspiring others. Whether you are at the helm of a large organization, guiding a small team, or simply striving to lead by example in your everyday life, the journey of leadership is one of the most challenging and rewarding paths you can embark on.

The stories, insights, and wisdom Michael shared in this book are your personal companions, a reference tool years in the formation. I hope this helps pave your way, challenge your assumptions, and inspire you to new heights of leadership.

Thank you, Michael, for allowing me the honor of sharing my thoughts, let the journey begin.

Christopher M. Allegretti, CPA
Managing Principal and CEO
HBK CPAs & Consultants

Acknowledgments

To my Dad. Your passion for leadership was infectious. I am forever grateful for the legacy you left in me. I miss you.

To my children—Zaiden, Quinn, Brinley, and Brogan. Always gain the leadership edge.

To my partners and team at HBK. Thank you for your ongoing belief and support. This book would not have been possible without you.

To Mike Shaw. Working with you on this book has been a great experience. You are a consummate professional and world-class writer. Thank you for your hard work and dedication.

An Introduction by Michael Ross

Through all my education, experience, and failures, I've settled on this truth: *Leadership is the most important business skill, hands down.*

The impact of leadership reverberates across every facet of an organization, shaping outcomes and driving success, as researchers have repeatedly determined:

- *Employees show up and work harder for good leaders.* Gallup studies reveal that 70 percent of an employee's engagement is determined by their immediate supervisor. Furthermore, companies with highly engaged employees outperform their competitors by an astounding 147 percent, and profitability is 21 percent greater when teams are highly engaged.

- *People leave bad leaders and stay with good leaders.* Leadership is a key factor in employee retention and satisfaction. Research by Salesforce indicates that employees who feel their voices are heard by their leaders are 4.6 times more likely to feel empowered to do their best work. Additionally, investing in employees' professional development has proven a wise strategy: 94 percent of employees are inclined to stay longer with a company that prioritizes their growth. Conversely, Gallup found that 75 percent of employees who voluntarily leave their jobs attribute their departures to their direct supervisors.

- *The better the leader, the better the performance.* Leadership also plays a pivotal role in enhancing productivity and performance in an organization. McKinsey discovered that companies implementing effective leadership practices achieve a fivefold higher return on investment. Moreover, the Society for Human Resource Management reports that 92 percent of employees believe their leaders' behavior directly impacts their job performance. With effective leadership, a team's productivity can improve by as much as 20 or 30 percent, according to Gallup.

- *Good leaders help people think outside the box and create better systems.* When it comes to fostering innovation and creativity, strong leadership is essential. Deloitte's research revealed that organizations with robust leadership and inclusive cultures are eight times more likely to achieve better business outcomes. An overwhelming 82 percent of employees consider a leader's ability to foster innovation crucial to the success of their organization, as highlighted by R&D provider InnoLead. However, Gallup's findings indicate only 51 percent of employees feel their leaders are doing enough to encourage creativity and innovation.

- *Better leadership equals more money and more sustainability.* Perhaps most notably, leadership impacts financial performance. McKinsey's research demonstrates that companies with gender-diverse leadership teams out-profit their peers by 25 percent. Additionally, leadership development, when done effectively, can lead to a remarkable 15 percent increase in earnings per share, according to Columbia Business School. And a study by Bain & Company involving 2,500 public companies found that those with strong leadership delivered a 10-year total shareholder return 3.5 times higher than companies with weak leadership.

Leadership is the linchpin of success in the business world. Its profound influence on employee engagement, retention, productivity, innovation, and financial performance underscores its indispensable nature. Organizations that are intentional in leadership development reap extraordinary benefits. But leading in today's dynamic business landscape is not easy. Business leaders from all levels and industries are confronting a host of new challenges that have surfaced or intensified in recent years. And it's important to note that these challenges aren't limited to those at the top of the corporate ladder. They impact leaders across various domains, such as construction leaders overseeing job sites, health care leaders balancing patient care and team management, and manufacturing leaders handling production, scheduling, and unexpected issues like supply chain interruptions. Uncertainty, volatility, and global crises are the new norm. Remote work, digital transformation, cybersecurity, AI, and DEI are just a few of what are now common challenges. Leaders must make strategic decisions, manage virtual teams, upskill their workforces, safeguard data, promote inclusivity, embrace sustainability, and protect their organizations' reputations. It's a complex balancing act.

The challenges, combined with ongoing responsibilities, demand strong leadership skills. Continuous learning and adaptability are key to thriving in such an ever-evolving landscape. The only way to stay afloat and outlast the competition is by developing strong leaders who can effectively guide their teams and organizations.

Due to the challenges, keen competition, and relentless change, developing leaders is no longer a luxury or optional investment; it is an imperative for businesses that want an edge. Businesses rise, fall, or stall based on their level of leadership. Regardless of industry or location, businesses that invest the time, energy, and resources to develop leaders in their organizations will enjoy a competitive edge. As well, by developing leaders who can develop other leaders, they will unleash the power of rapid and sustainable growth. After all, business is simply people buying, selling, and trading goods and services for something of equal value. If an organization can develop people with the skills to put people, team members, and customers in the best position to succeed, it is easy to see that they themselves will be successful.

But if a business does not develop leaders, if they choose to stay at their level of leadership or continue in mediocrity, they will crumble. Good leaders attract good customers and team members. Poor leaders attract poor customers and team members.

Gaining *a* leadership edge begins with accepting the fact that leadership is the most important business skill, then being intentional about investing in leadership development and creating a culture of leadership development.

The leadership edge is the only true edge in the marketplace. Products and services will become obsolete, systems will fail, and trends will expire.

Organizations with people who have the skills, knowledge, and efficacy to lead will always have an edge regardless of market fluctuations. Through investing in leadership development, organizations unlock the hidden potential within their workforce; they turn challenges into opportunities, create a robust leadership pipeline, go from limitations to limitlessness, and cultivate a strong, adaptable, and forward-thinking culture.

It's important to note that leadership, as with any other skill, is best acquired with the help of trained professionals. If you wanted to master the piano, you would save yourself a lot of time and make much better progress by taking lessons from a credentialed teacher. Experienced, results-oriented leadership coaches, consultants, and trainers will help you master your leadership skills.

Through my education and experience, I have learned that anyone who *wants* to become a great leader *can* become a great leader. Leadership is not restricted to people with certain natural abilities that magically springboard them to influence, prestige, and greatness. It is circumscribed, however, to people who decide they are going to go against the status quo, push their limits, and influence others to do the same. Let it be clear: Developing in leadership is challenging. It is also an ongoing life-long pursuit. No matter how far you go in your leadership journey, there will always be more to learn and more room for improvement.

I wrote The Leadership Edge to give business leaders and leadership coaches, consultants, and trainers the framework for developing strong business leaders who can learn to develop other strong business leaders. This book will serve as a guide, offering insights, strategies, and practical tools to empower individuals and organizations to gain a leadership edge. Whether you are a seasoned executive, a middle manager, an emerging leader, or a leadership consultant, the principles and practices explored here will give you the knowledge and resources to unleash your leadership potential and make a meaningful impact on the organizations you work in.

In Part 1, *The Foundations of Leadership Development*, you will learn why leadership development programs fail and how to fix them. We discuss the origins, definition, and purpose of leadership, then talk about the importance of understanding free market and business systems. And we cover the PVD (purpose, vision, discipline) system, which is a foundation of thinking, behaving, and communicating as an effective leader both on a macro and micro scale.

In Part 2, *Leadership Development Disciplines*, we discuss effective leadership disciplines such as self-leadership, verbal and nonverbal communication, and the ways successful business leaders think, behave, and connect with others. We address topics such as systems thinking, emotional intelligence, conflict management, and relationship building.

In Part 3, *Building a Culture of Leadership Development*, we discuss strategies for fostering collaboration, nurturing talent, and cultivating a culture of continuous learning that leads to sustainable and systematic growth.

As you embark on this journey, be prepared to challenge your assumptions, embrace new perspectives, and explore practical strategies for nurturing and empowering leaders within your organization. Together we will unlock the transformative power of leadership development and shape a future where exceptional leaders pave the way for others, both within your organization and beyond.

Let's gain The Leadership Edge.

PART 1

The Foundations of Leadership Development

CHAPTER 1

Foundation #1

Why Leadership Development Programs Fail

It was my third Zoom consultation of the day. I was meeting with three partners of a health care company. Each of the partners was a doctor, each with a different specialization. All three saw numerous patients daily while attempting to handle the leadership duties necessary to run a successful business. They explained the leadership and culture challenges they had been facing, and before I had a chance to respond, one of the partners posed what I interpreted as half confession and half accusation: "We were hesitant to meet with you. You see, we've invested in leadership development programs before, and to be honest, we saw very little change."

I'd heard it before. I thanked the partner for her honesty, and then asked about the programs they'd used. How involved were the doctors? What were their expectations prior to investing in the programs? What accountability mechanisms did they use?

There were a few nationally known one-week programs and a couple of online courses they passed along to other people in their firm whose leadership they needed to run a successful business. However, they had not established clear expectations of those prospective leaders, nor did they follow up to see how they were applying what they were learning.

The programs they had invested in were doomed to failure. They did not have the systematic elements for leadership development. Nor were the doctors/partners sufficiently involved. Even if a program was excellent, I told them, they would see little to no change, certainly nothing sustainable. I added, "Leadership development is one of the most important and most difficult undertakings in business. It's hard work that requires strict intentionality."

In order for their business to work well, they had to find a way to develop leaders who could run the business while they worked as health care providers. I explained how leaders could be put in the best position to grow and develop, and how they could empower them. We discussed plans and approaches in detail, and when we had finalized our plans, we went to work.

Over the following two years, we developed leaders who took ownership of their marketing, sales, operations, and administration departments. They grew their top line by more than 25 percent, their bottom line ballooned, stress and turnover levels decreased, and they reported a happier workforce.

It was not a quick fix. In leadership development, there is no quick fix.

A Soft Skill?

I've always found it interesting that leadership is categorized as a "soft" skill. I know that characterization is not meant to imply that leadership is not important, but words matter. Soft implies weak, mushy, sloppy, gushy, and fluffy. None of those words describes the great leaders I've been around or studied for the past 20 years. Human beings are complex creatures; the number of variables that influence the way just two people think, behave, and communicate with each other is infinite. Getting an entire group of people to work together toward the same purpose, vision, and discipline is hard, so hard that many in leadership positions settle for less because the task of unification is one of the most difficult challenges anyone can face. It's much harder than the "hard" skills, like finance, administration, logistics, and technology. In fact, effective leaders must be proficient in those hard skills as well as able to guide, direct, protect, and correct their teams.

If you're soft, you cannot lead. You have to be powerful. You must be willing to engage in challenge, contrast, and conflict while influencing people to stay connected, unified, and purpose-driven. And organizations have to be willing to lean into the pain, challenges, and time it takes to develop strong leaders.

Most organizations do not understand how hard it is to lead, to become an effective leader. Subsequently, they fail when it comes to developing people who can drive change and growth. Not that they don't try. Globally, companies are spending nearly $400 billion annually on leadership development. Yet data provided by McKinsey[1] offers startling insight into the industry: *Most leadership programs fail to create real and lasting impact.* Barbara Kellerman points this out in detail in *The End of Leadership.* She says, "The leadership industry deficits loom large. Instead of making our leaders more effective and ethical, it seems at least to have had the opposite effect—it seems to have made things worse."[2]

Statistics support her:

- Globally, 85 percent of employees are either not engaged or actively disengaged at work.[3] As we mentioned in our "Introduction," leadership accounts for 70 percent of the variance in team engagement.
- 21 percent of employees disagree or strongly disagree that their leader would do what is right if they raised a concern about ethics and integrity.[4]
- 50 percent of employees who have quit their jobs said they left to get away from their manager.[5]
- 79 percent of employees say they feel a "lack of appreciation" from their leaders.[6]
- 91 percent of employees say their leaders lack the ability to communicate well.[7]
- More than 80 percent of leadership positions are filled by internal promotion,[8] and 91 percent of leaders say they were not properly trained to lead.[9]

All the investment in leadership development netting little to no change leaves employees and leaders frustrated, cynical, and sometimes even hostile toward those in the leadership industry. It has frustrated my team, as we are often met with cynicism from potential clients or categorized as motivational speakers offering little or no substance. In any industry, you'll find people who don't deliver on their promises. The leadership industry is no exception. Now, I do not believe this is intentional on the part of leadership development companies or leadership trainers, coaches, and consultants.

Seven Insights on Why Leadership Programs Fail

The experiences of more than 15 years of training leaders, many more years of business ownership and practical leadership, and countless hours and dollars invested in leadership programs have taught me why many leadership programs fail to produce better leaders.

Insight #1

Programs focus on character development as opposed to leadership development. One problem with the leadership industry is that it generally focuses on character development. Books, trainings, and seminars promote character traits like hard work, perseverance, positive attitude, and integrity. Of course, good character is essential to leadership. It affects how leaders treat others. It helps leaders make better decisions. It builds trust between leaders and followers. And it sustains leaders in times of crisis. However, leadership is a *multidisciplinary skill.* I know a lot of men and women with good character who are not good leaders. They treat people well, want people to succeed, and support people as they do their work. But when it comes to unifying teams toward a common direction, communicating effectively, holding people accountable, and producing results, they fall short.

Leaders should be people of high moral character. Character is essential for maintaining success. But it is not alone sufficient to lead a team of people. Leaders must develop a plethora of skills, such as vision and goal setting, prioritization, communication, problem-solving, negotiation, facilitation, conflict management, scheduling, delegation, strategic thinking, and strategic planning.

To reemphasize: Leadership is a multidisciplinary skill. Good character is foundational, but without the full complement of essential leadership skills, leaders' effectiveness will be limited.

Insight #2

Business success stories do not equate to sound leadership development. Another misconception about leadership is found in content produced by business people who believe they can teach leadership because they've been successful in business. They write books, speak, do interviews, and share their success stories as a model for others to follow. The material is inspiring because most of them started with very little and through hard work and perseverance overcame adversity, created great wealth, and positively impacted others. However, other than inspiration, their stories are of little use in helping people transform into strong leaders. Most often, they are narratives peppered with truisms they learned on their personal journeys.

There's no one-size-fits-all approach to leadership. On the contrary, it's one-size-fits-one. Every leader is unique in personality, physical attributes, mannerisms, experiences, and education. Many of the business people writing about leadership take the do-it-like-me approach and do not consider the variables. Imagine LeBron James writing a book about his successes as a basketball player. Due to his celebrity, many people would buy his book, and certainly, his story would be inspiring, including lessons about believing in your dreams and never giving up. But if he instructed people to play the way he played, relying on a 48-in. vertical leap to soar over an opponent and slam dunk or bullying an opponent who is a mere 6 ft. 6 in. and 220 pounds, it wouldn't be very helpful to a youngster trying out for his sixth-grade team. Better to turn to instructional leadership offered by individuals who have studied and practiced how to develop successful leaders through systematic-based and behavioral science-based approaches.

Leadership development must be focused on helping leaders become aware of their unique talents, personality, and abilities, and giving them a framework for using them. Do-it-like-me leadership hurts more than it helps because people trying to follow the model inevitably find that the model works only for the person who lived it. And when it fails for them, they lose resolve and confidence.

Insight #3

Many leadership programs are poorly designed. Leadership development, growth, and change do not happen by accident. They require the application of specific processes and sequences rooted in strict intentionality.

Most people I've met in my industry are good, smart, and motivated people who authentically want to help leaders. Most have good material that when applied can make a substantial difference in leaders' lives. However, many of their programs suffer from design flaws passed down to them by people who used programs with flawed designs in their training. Poor programs equal poor results. Poor design equals poor results in leadership development equals poor leadership equals poor employee performance.

Insight #4

Programs can lack top-down vision, expectations, and involvement. Leadership development programs must be conducted intentionally toward a specific end. As I tell my clients, "If you want this program to work, it must be woven into the fabric of your organization." To be successful, a leadership program needs the involvement and commitment of top management. Most organizations understand how important leadership development is, but, given other pressing demands, they often fail to dedicate the time to leadership development that it requires. So they often turn to their human resource directors to look for external programs that can accommodate their busy schedules. They find a few, interview the potential vendors, pick one, and send off their people expecting them to return better leaders.

It can work for a while. Those who go through the program return energized and motivated, with new leadership tools. But after a month or two, the energy runs out, the motivation plummets, and those tools are stuffed away on a metaphoric shelf to begin collecting dust. Why? Because too often, when top-level leaders enroll their people in leadership programs, they do not clearly articulate the reasons, the vision for why they put them in the program, and their expectations for their development. Worse, they're not involved, even from a position of oversight.

Leadership development is meant to improve skills, broaden mindsets, and resolve leadership deficiencies within an organization. Without a clear vision, goals, and involvement from the top, the program cannot be woven into the fabric of an organization. People who go through the programs often return with a plethora of leadership tools, confidence, efficacy, and skills that don't get used to their potential.

Insight #5

Programs often fail to measure and evaluate. You can't manage what you don't measure. Without proper measurement and evaluation, you can't determine the effectiveness of a leadership development program. Leadership programs should have clear evaluation metrics and methods to assess the impact of the program on leaders' performance and related business outcomes. That feedback loop is essential for identifying areas of improvement and making necessary adjustments to the program.

Senior leadership must be clear about the vision, goals, and growth expectations for anyone they enroll in a program. They must communicate those expectations to the leadership expert facilitating their program. A shotgun approach to leadership development might touch on myriad key points, but it's much more effective to be clear about where you want to see development, even if it's relegated to one area.

Insight #6

Many organizations don't follow effective promotion strategies. As mentioned earlier, more than 80 percent of promotions are internal. Typically those individuals are promoted to leadership positions based on their performance and technical competency.

When employees consistently demonstrate outstanding competency, exceed performance expectations, and achieve significant results, it is natural to consider them for promotion. That recognition serves as a reward for their hard work, dedication, and ability to consistently deliver exceptional outcomes. Promoting individuals based on their performance motivates employees, reinforces a culture of excellence, and encourages others to strive for similar levels of success. But technical competence and performance are not the best reasons for moving an employee into a position of leadership where they will be expected to teach, guide, train, mentor, admonish, and evaluate others. A person considered for a leadership position must be able to demonstrate that they can duplicate their success through others. Still, leadership competencies are often overlooked, and people are promoted prematurely, which results in frustrations for the new leader and the people they are assigned to lead.

Insight #7

Program participants lack holistic business understanding. We have seen many people coming into our leadership programs who lack a basic understanding of how their organization works. They might understand how to do their jobs, they know how to accomplish day-to-day tasks, and they understand the importance of improving basic leadership competencies. But many do not understand *why* they are doing their job and how vital it is to the overall business operation. Their lack of understanding of how their job affects other components of the business results in a lack of intentionality in communication, initiative, and continuous improvement. Consider the adage: A manager knows how a leader knows why and how. Positional leaders must have an understanding of how the business works so they can work proactively and produce real results.

I'm not proposing that these insights and observations make for a comprehensive list of reasons leadership programs fail to generate results, but they are the reasons I've seen most frequently. In fact, I learned how to create programs that make for real and lasting leadership change and growth after making some of these mistakes. I tested many programs and theories on my own businesses and with a few very gracious clients, and through trial and error, validity and falsifiability, and resolve and rigor, learned what it takes to produce real results in leadership development.

Seven Elements of a Successful Leadership Development Program

Successful leadership development programs must address seven factors or elements. If a course does not offer all seven, it might not be a bad program, but it won't be sufficiently comprehensive. Be sure to do your due diligence before diving into a program that will leave you frustrated.

1. *Resolve:* Leaders must have the resolve to change, grow, and lead others. If someone does not want to change, they will not change. It does not matter how dynamic the speaker, trainer, or coach is. It's a waste of time and money to force a person into a program they don't want to be in. They must want to engage and do what is necessary to improve.

2. *Rigor:* Rigor produces character, which is a foundation of great leadership. If the course doesn't challenge, push, and stretch, it's a waste of time and money. Skills are hard to develop. It takes a great deal of hard work, rigor, and discipline to become an excellent leader.

3. *Relevance:* Development programs should be relevant to the leader's environment. As explained earlier, the program must be woven into the fabric of the organization where a person leads. If the training does not have relevance, the leaders will not apply the lessons, and it will be a waste of time and resources. The best leadership programs are intentional in ensuring relevance, and the trainers are loath to engage with an organization that has not been clear about relevance for those participating in the program. It is the application of our education that creates change; without relevance there can be no application.

4. *Relationships:* Courses should encourage and facilitate relationships among the participants. Relationships give leaders a chance to look at theories from multiple perspectives. They help leaders continue the leadership discourse long after the course. Many courses consider building relationships among participants a key element.

5. *Longevity:* Research shows that behavioral change does not last unless a person goes through at least six months of focusing on making that change a habit. Many leadership programs seek to accommodate people's busy lifestyles, but less time-intensive programs are also less effective.

6. *Frequency:* Research shows that one touch per week—combined with the six months of longevity—keeps trainees focused on change. This does not require class time, but it does mean that there should be a weekly activity, coaching session, or interaction. Technological advances have made it easier to achieve and maintain frequency.

7. *Accountability:* If the leadership course does not have standards and guidelines, it will not have accountability. Three ways courses should hold participants accountable:

i. Requirements: If a person does not fulfill the course's requirements, they should not get certification upon completing the course. Requirements can include attendance, assignments, coaching sessions, and presentations. If the person is not keeping up with course requirements during the program, they should be considered for removal. A person who is not engaged diminishes the value of the experience for those who are.

ii. Testing: Testing creates accountability. Writing assignments test what a person is learning with less pressure than a formal test. Formal testing is a way to ensure the material covered will be remembered and can be recalled.

iii. Demonstration: Leaders need to be able to give presentations, speak clearly, and think logically about leadership theories. A presentation requires a person to do all three—and it helps a leader overcome the fear of public speaking.

A leadership development program worth its salt holds participants accountable. Accountability is vital for leadership development and little change will occur without it.

A final note on chapter 1: Leadership development programs must include all seven elements of an effective program to provide for lasting change. If you've completed a program that didn't include all seven, you can at least use the seven as a guide and strategic framework for filling in the gaps. Moreover, use the seven insights on why programs fail and the seven elements of a successful program as you consider investing in a program. While people offering leadership training generally and genuinely care about helping leaders develop, many lack the education, experience, and substance to build and lead programs that create real and lasting change. It can be easy to buy into a program based on an infectious personality, but if the program is built to fail, it will fail regardless of the heart and energy of that person.

Chapter 1 Takeaways

- Leadership development is one of the most important and most difficult undertakings in business. It's hard work that requires strict intentionality.
- Many leadership development programs are designed not to work.
- Getting an entire group of people to work together toward the same purpose, vision, and discipline is hard, so hard that many in leadership positions settle for less because the task of unification is one of the most difficult challenges anyone can face.
- You must be willing to engage in challenge, contrast, and conflict while influencing people to stay connected, unified, and purpose-driven.
- All the investment in leadership development netting little to no change leaves employees and leaders frustrated, cynical, and sometimes even hostile toward those in the leadership industry.
- Leadership is a multidisciplinary skill. Good character is foundational, but without the full complement of essential leadership skills, leaders' effectiveness will be limited.
- Without a clear vision, goals, and involvement from the top, a leadership program cannot be woven into the fabric of an organization.
- A person considered for a leadership position must be able to demonstrate that they can duplicate their success through others.
- A manager knows how a leader knows why and how.
- Successful leadership development programs must address seven factors: resolve, rigor, relevance, relationships, longevity, frequency, and accountability.

CHAPTER 2

Foundation #2

Defining Leadership and Understanding Its Purpose and Vision

Once your program is structured for success, you can begin to add the other foundational pieces, starting with defining leadership and understanding its purpose and vision.

At the beginning of our leadership development programs, we ask participants to write down their definitions of leadership. We assure them that there are no right or wrong answers. After they complete the initial writing portion of the exercise, we pair them with other members of the group and have them share their definitions. Once they complete their discussion, we give them an opportunity to make changes to their definition based on the sharing. Then we debrief with them as a group and ask them to share their original and altered definitions. Nearly every time, participants change their definitions after their discussions with others, an indication that they did not originally have a clear understanding of leadership, or, for that matter, its application.

That is significant because *belief is the precedent of all action*. A person's belief about leadership will fundamentally affect how they lead. And if someone is not clear about their definition of leadership, they cannot be intentional in the way they lead.

To develop any skill or capability, a person must start with a solid foundation. A solid foundation of leadership starts with understanding its meaning, its purpose, and how to fulfill its purpose in context and intentionality.

Origins

The word leadership has its origins in Old English. It is derived from the word *lǣdan*, which means to lead or to guide. Over time, this word evolved into *lēod* or lēodscipe, which referred to the state or condition of being a leader.

The word leadership itself emerged in the English language during the 19th century, combining the root lead with the suffix "-ership," indicating the state or position of being a leader. The term gained prominence as a way to describe the act, skill, or ability of guiding, directing, or influencing others in a group or organization.

The concept of leadership, however, predates the actual word. Throughout history, individuals have assumed leadership roles in various social, political, and organizational contexts. Leadership has been a constant throughout civilization, with leaders providing guidance, making decisions, and inspiring others to achieve common goals.

Different cultures and societies have had their own concepts of and terms for leadership. The ancient Greek concept *archon* referred to a leader or ruler. The Chinese term *junzi* denoted a virtuous and noble leader. These examples illustrate the universal need for leadership and the recognition of its importance in human societies.

Today, the term leadership encompasses a wide range of theories, styles, and practices. It involves the ability to influence, motivate, and inspire others to work toward a shared vision or goal. Leadership is studied in fields such as psychology, management, and organizational behavior, wherein numerous theories and models have been developed to understand its dynamics and efficacy.

In summary, while the word leadership has relatively recent origins in the English language, the concept of leading and guiding others has been an integral part of human history and is essential for the functioning of organizations and communities.

Expanding on the Definition

In *Leadership for the Twenty-First Century*,[1] Dr. Joseph Rost examined hundreds of leadership definitions by 20th-century scholars, organizational leaders, and philosophers. He concluded by attempting to summarize his findings of the essence of leadership in a singular definition: "Leadership is an influence relationship between leaders and followers that intends real changes based upon mutual purposes."

Rost's definition includes intentional and well-placed keywords such as influence, relationships, change, and purpose. To fully grasp the concept of leadership, each must be analyzed.

- *Leadership is influence.* Influence is defined as "the capacity to have an effect on the character, development, or behavior of someone or something, or the effect itself." When promoted to a position of leadership, a person is given a platform for exerting influence at a higher level, but a leader will only maintain their influence if they know, understand, and use their platform to guide, inspire, admonish, teach, and create positive results both for the individuals they are leading and for their organization holistically.

- *Leadership is built on relationships.* My dad loved the saying, "Relationships are the bridges over which values are transferred." To maintain and perpetuate influence, leaders must build relationships with their team members. They must be intentional about getting to know their team members on a personal and professional level. They must know what is important to them, what their goals are, what their challenges are, and what motivates them. This is something we will build upon here in *The Leadership Edge*, but suffice it to say for now that relationship building is a skill that must be mastered if a leader desires better results.

- *Leadership is about change.* Leaders consistently look for better ways to do things. They are never satisfied with the status quo. They always believe that things can be done more effectively, efficiently, and effortlessly. Great leaders always ask, "How can we achieve more with less time and fewer resources?" The platitude "if you're not changing you are not growing" is true, and true leaders embrace change and are intentional in creating it.

- *Leadership is about mutual purposes.* Every leader must know the purpose of their organization, the purpose of leadership, and the purpose of each team member's responsibilities relative to their organization's purpose. Purpose starts with understanding why something exists, but purpose is maintained by being purposeful in action. Leaders lead from a purpose and with a purpose. Without clearly identifying and being intentional with purpose, a leader's efforts will fall short.
- *Leading with purpose requires leaders to:*
  o Lead with vision and direction: At its core, leadership serves as a guiding force, providing a clear vision and direction for individuals, teams, and organizations. A leader's ability to articulate a compelling vision that resonates with others ignites a sense of purpose and motivates individuals to work toward a common goal. By setting a direction and outlining a roadmap to success, leaders empower their followers to align their efforts, make informed decisions, and complex challenges.
  o Inspire and motivate: One of the main purposes of leadership is to inspire and motivate others to achieve their full potential. A true leader understands the unique strengths and talents of their team members and empowers them to leverage those attributes effectively. By providing guidance, support, and encouragement, leaders create an environment where individuals feel motivated, valued, and empowered to excel. They foster a culture of collaboration, innovation, and continuous growth, thereby driving individual and collective achievement.
  o Facilitate growth and development: Leadership is instrumental in facilitating personal and professional growth. Effective leaders identify and nurture talent, providing opportunities for skill development, learning,

and advancement. They invest in mentorship and coaching, guiding individuals to overcome obstacles, enhance their capabilities, and reach new heights of achievement. Through constructive feedback and recognition, leaders create an environment conducive to continuous improvement and the realization of untapped potential.

o Drive change and innovation: Leadership is closely intertwined with change and innovation. In today's rapidly evolving world, leaders must possess the ability to adapt, embrace new ideas, and lead their teams on transformational journeys. They challenge the status quo, foster a culture of creativity and risk-taking, and inspire others to embrace change as an opportunity for growth. By driving innovation, including embracing emerging technologies, leaders position their organizations at the forefront of progress and create sustainable competitive advantages.

o Build trust and collaboration: Leadership plays a vital role in establishing trust and fostering collaboration among individuals and within teams. Trust is a cornerstone of effective leadership, as it creates an environment of psychological safety, open communication, and mutual respect. By leading with integrity, transparency, and empathy, leaders cultivate trust and inspire loyalty. They encourage collaboration, break down silos, and harness the collective intelligence of their teams, leading to improved problem-solving, innovation, and overall organizational performance.

By leading with purpose, leaders can shape a better future, empower others to excel, and leave a lasting legacy of positive change. However, to comprehensively capitalize on the power of purpose, leadership must have a vision.

The Vision of Leadership

The overarching vision of leadership is *to improve the quality of life for humankind.* According to Dr. Phil Stutz, there are three certainties in life:

1. *Pain:* People experience various types of pain during their lives, including physical, emotional, social, existential, psychological, spiritual, and chronic. Almost every day people experience any or all of these types of pains.
2. *Uncertainty:* Uncertainty is a common and inevitable part of life, and people encounter it in various aspects of their personal, professional, and social spheres. We deal with uncertainty in such areas as our decision making, our social-political lives, our job or business, technology, relationships, environment, and health. Uncertainty can leave us with feelings of ambiguity and insecurity.
3. *The need for constant work:* No matter how many times you pull weeds from your garden, the weeds will return. No matter how many times you eat, you will become hungry again. No matter how many times you solve a problem, another problem emerges. The need for constant work is woven into the fabric of life because there is always something to be done, something to be addressed, and something to be accomplished or resolved.

Leaders should never ignore the three certainties of life. Rather, they should accept and celebrate them as opportunities to improve the quality of life for their customers and team members. Visionary leaders discover ways to alleviate pain and create pleasure, create certainty in the face of uncertainty for as many people as possible, and turn the need for constant work into opportunities to work efficiently and effectively. Leaders are able to do so by first becoming extremely clear about the results they want to create.

Vision is often misunderstood as a broad, intangible, and unreachable idea that acts as a carrot on a stick to keep people striving. Vision is neither broad nor obscure. It is clear, measurable, and tangible, an understanding of the future as it could and should be: free of pain, uncertainty, and the need for constant work, if only for a time.

Consider the following vision for your body in light of Dr. Stutz's three certainties: You feel pain; have uncertainty knowing that if you don't do something you could have a serious physical breakdown; and understand that if you don't lean into constant work and become intentional about your health, you will have to settle for the unhealthy body you don't want. So you set about clarifying your vision of a healthy body by:

- Looking in the mirror and envisioning your body as you want it to be.
- Taking account of areas of your body where you'd like to lose inches or pounds.
- Calculating your body mass index (BMI) and identifying what it should be.
- Assessing where you want better muscle definition and where you want less cellulite.
- For inspiration and ongoing stimulation, finding pictures of people who look like you want to look and putting them in places where you will see them often.
- Stepping on a scale and determining how much weight you want to lose.
- Determining a time frame: how long it will take to lose those pounds and inches, decrease BMI, increase muscle definition, and decrease cellulite.

Your vision for your body is now clear, and you are ready to live from a purpose and with a purpose.

Vision sets leadership in motion. It is how leaders can be purposeful and intentional. Without clarity of vision, leaders will be listless, ineffective, and frustrated. It is the responsibility of every leader to make sure they are clear about the results they expect and that are expected of them. A simple way to determine whether or not a vision is clear is to ask, "How will I measure whether or not the vision is achieved?" In our example, you could step on a scale to learn whether or not you've lost pounds, you could measure your waist, you could assess your BMI, and you could compare and contrast your body image with the pictures you have posted around you.

Leaders want to create a better quality of life for their organizations and people, including themselves. Therefore, a leader must be clear about the results they want to create or are expected to create. But even if they lose clarity, a leader can always look for ways to alleviate pain, decrease uncertainty, and be more effective and efficient with their constant work.

Business Leadership

We now turn our attention to discussing leadership in terms of how it functions in business, which is the focus of my work, consulting with business leaders and helping them develop their skills, character, and efficacy.

Context in leadership is key. How effective a leader can be is largely determined by the context in which they're leading. A leader who is skilled in coaching hockey will not be as effective coaching a debate team; they would at least need to understand the rules of debate to be effective in influencing their team toward change for mutual purpose and vision.

Effective business leaders must fully understand the rules of the "game" they are playing, starting with the free market system.

Chapter 2 Takeaways

- A solid foundation of leadership starts with understanding its meaning, its purpose, and how to fulfill its purpose in context and intentionality.
- As defined by Dr. Joseph Rost, "Leadership is an influence relationship between leaders and followers that intends real changes based upon mutual purposes."
- Relationship building is a skill that must be mastered if a leader desires better results.
- A leader's ability to articulate a compelling vision that resonates with others ignites a sense of purpose and motivates individuals to work toward a common goal.
- A true leader understands the unique strengths and talents of their team members and empowers them to leverage those attributes effectively.

- Leaders should accept and celebrate the three certainties of life—pain, uncertainty, and the need for constant work—as opportunities to improve the quality of life for their customers and team members.
- Vision sets leadership in motion. It is how leaders can be purposeful and intentional.

CHAPTER 3

Foundation #3

Understanding the Rules of a Free-Market System

Jade was a bright youngster who knew at an early age that she would be a business owner one day. At 11, she began on her career path with a yard sale. She took a wagon around her neighborhood and asked people if they had clothes, shoes, or other items they wanted to get rid of. Most were delighted to comply. Jade took many trips and filled her wagon multiple times.

With the help of her friends Jordan and Tamara, Jade arranged the items by category and set up a shop in her yard. The three created a dozen "yard sale" signs to post around the neighborhood, made a stack of flyers to take to local stores, and put multiple posts on Facebook announcing the date, time, location, and items for sale.

On the day of the yard sale, Jade, Jordan, and Tamara set up a drink and snack stand, a check-out table for taking payments, and another table with a sign that read "Q&A" where Jade would answer questions about the items for sale.

The weather was perfect, and traffic was steady throughout the day. Many people from the neighborhood came and bought the items Jade had collected from their neighbors. They sold out of snacks and more than three-fourths of the items for a total of $854. Jade gave Jordan and Tamara each $200 for their efforts; they were ecstatic.

Jade put aside the rest of her take and began looking for ways to reinvest. She had a passion for animals, had pet-sat for several of her neighbors, and decided her next venture would be grooming cats and dogs. She spent $150 to buy grooming equipment and another $250 on a grooming course, where she was given workbooks, an instruction guide, and video training. She read and watched the material until she felt comfortable enough to get started.

Jade's parents gave her permission to set up an area in their garage to do the grooming. She organized the area and started her marketing campaign: flyers to local grocery stores, street signs, and calls to her pet-sitting customers.

Business was slow for the first few months, with an average of only two pets per week. Jade wasn't making much money, but she focused on doing the best job she could for the customers she had. She reviewed her course materials frequently and asked for feedback on her work from her customers. Her skills improved.

One of her customers, a dog breeder, noticed Jade's improved skills, her determination, and how she cared for the animals and about her customers' satisfaction. She began referring her customers to Jade, and in a couple of months, Jade's business had grown to more than 10 bookings per week. She again recruited her friends Jordan and Tamara and trained them on the grooming process, and they began working to improve their skills. The requests and bookings continued to increase, and soon Jade, Jordan, and Tamara were each averaging more than 10 groomings per week. They recruited more friends, and the business grew.

Today, Jade owns 13 animal day cares that include grooming services, on-call vet services, and her own line of organic pet food. She employs over 100 people and has been intentional about hiring people who share her passion for animal care. Her story is a classic example of how free-market economic systems work and how anyone with an idea that brings value to the marketplace can start a business and multiply value by hiring and training passionate people.

Understanding the Free Market and Its Rules

A free-market system is an economic system where the prices of goods and services are determined by supply and demand in the marketplace without significant intervention from the government or other external forces. It is characterized by private ownership, voluntary exchange, competition, and limited government interference.

In simple terms, the free market is where *people* buy, sell, and trade goods and services for an agreed-upon exchange of value with limited government interference. I emphasize *people* because they must follow the rules of the system for it to work. Leadership involves intentionally putting people in the best position to succeed; the only way to do this effectively in business is to understand the rules of the system you're leading in.

One of the most important aspects of becoming an effective business leader in a free-market system is understanding how the system works, that is, the rules. Just as a sports coach needs to understand the rules of the sport to guide, mentor, train, teach, and position their team for success, a business leader needs to take the same approach in a free-market system. By doing so, they will be able to think holistically about how their decisions affect their organization and how to communicate effectively with their teams. The interpersonal skills taught by the vast majority of leadership development programs are valuable but will have limited effectiveness without applying them to the fundamentals and rules of a free-market system.

I often tell my clients that instead of fighting "what is," they need to become good at understanding and working with "what is." Effective leaders don't spend a lot of time complaining about reality; they accept it and use it to their advantage—and they look for opportunity in adversity. Rules are a set of explicit or understood regulations or principles governing conduct within a particular activity or sphere. Understanding the rules of free-market systems empowers leaders to be proactive in the way they think, behave, and communicate.

A few important rules of free-market economic systems are shown next.

Rule #1

Private ownership: In a free-market system, any individual or group of individuals has the right to own and control property, including resources, land, products, proprietary services, and means of production. Private ownership allows individuals to make decisions about how they spend money and use their resources based on their own interests and market signals.

Example: Sarah owns a small boutique shop in the city. She handpicks unique clothing and accessories to sell in her store. As a sole owner, Sarah has complete control over operations. She determines the pricing, selects inventory, and manages the day-to-day affairs. Any profits earned from the business belong to Sarah as the private owner, allowing her to reinvest in the store's growth or use them for personal reasons. Private ownership enables Sarah to pursue her entrepreneurial passion and shape her business according to her vision and goals.

Rule #2

Voluntary exchange: Participants in a free-market system engage in voluntary transactions. Buyers and sellers freely enter into agreements to exchange goods, services, or resources based on mutually agreed-upon terms. Both parties benefit from the exchange, as they acquire something they value more than what they give up.

Example: John wants to buy a new laptop, and Mary owns an electronics store. John visits Mary's store and finds a laptop that meets his needs. They engage in a voluntary exchange: John offers to pay the listed price, and Mary agrees to sell the laptop to him. Both parties willingly participate in the transaction based on their own preferences and perceived value. John obtains the laptop, and Mary receives payment for the sale. Voluntary exchange in a free-market system allows individuals to freely engage in transactions based on mutual consent.

Rule #3

Competition: Every market has multiple producers and sellers competing to attract customers and generate profits. Competition motivates businesses to improve their products, services, or prices to gain an edge. It drives innovation, efficiency, and quality improvements, all of which benefit consumers.

Example: In a bustling neighborhood, there are several coffee shops. Each shop strives to stand out. One coffee shop offers organic and fair-trade coffee, another focuses on unique blends, and a third emphasizes a cozy atmosphere. They all offer competitive prices, loyalty programs, and excellent customer service, and the competition encourages innovation and quality products and services. Their vibrant market environment benefits consumers who have a variety of options and pushes the shops to constantly improve and deliver value in order to stay competitive.

Rule #4

Price determination: Prices of goods and services in a free-market system are determined by supply and demand. When demand for a product or service exceeds supply, the price tends to rise. When supply exceeds demand, prices tend to fall. The mechanism serves to allocate resources efficiently and signals producers to adjust their production levels accordingly.

Example: Vendors in a farmers market sell fresh fruits. When there is an abundant supply of a particular fruit, say apples, and fewer buyers, the price of apples decreases as apple sellers compete. But if there is a limited supply of rare fruit, say dragon fruit, and high demand, the price of dragon fruit increases. In a free-market system, prices fluctuate based on the market's conditions and the interests of buyers and sellers.

Rule #5

Profit motive: In a free-market system, individuals and businesses are motivated by profit. By providing goods or services that consumers value, businesses can generate revenue exceeding their costs and earn profits. The profit motive encourages entrepreneurship, risk-taking, and investment, driving economic growth and innovation. The profit motive also provides for the research and development of new products and services, which often translates into more jobs.

Example: Samantha is an entrepreneur who starts her own bakery. She bakes delicious pastries, carefully manages costs, and sets competitive prices. Samantha constantly looks for ways to improve efficiency, attract more customers, and increase sales. Her profit motive drives her to innovate by introducing new flavors, offering customized cakes, and exploring partnerships with local cafes. The profits earned from the bakery not only reward Samantha for her hard work, but they also allow her to reinvest in the business, expanding, hiring more staff, and ultimately achieving her long-term financial goals. The profit motive in a free-market system serves as a powerful incentive for entrepreneurs like Samantha to take risks, create value, and drive economic growth.

Rule #6

Limited government intervention: Free-market economic systems are characterized by limited government interference. While the government plays a role in maintaining law and order, enforcing contracts, protecting property rights, and preventing monopolistic practices or fraud, it generally avoids excessive regulation or control over the economy. "Free" allows the market to function based on individual choices and voluntary interactions. When and where governments intervene excessively, markets are less free and there is a subsequent decrease in innovation and creativity.

Example: Government may establish laws and regulations that prevent businesses from engaging in fraudulent activities or anticompetitive practices. It may also set standards for consumer protection and product safety. But beyond providing these protections, government does not interfere with the day-to-day operations of businesses in a true free-market system. It does not dictate prices, production levels, or market entry. Businesses and individuals make economic decisions based on their own judgment; government fosters an environment of entrepreneurship, innovation, and individual freedom.

Rule #7

Consumer sovereignty: In a free-market system, consumers determine which goods and services succeed or fail through their purchasing decisions. They choose what to buy based on their preferences, needs, and budget. Producers, in turn, respond to consumer demand and adjust production accordingly.

Example: Consumers choose a smartphone brand based on its features, their budget, and their uses or needs. When one brand consistently offers better features, durability, and value, consumers gravitate to it, and the brand's market share increases. As a result, a competing brand will be motivated to improve its offerings to regain consumer favor. Consumer sovereignty drives businesses to prioritize customer satisfaction, quality, and innovation to attract and retain customers in a competitive marketplace.

Rule #8

Spontaneous order: A free-market system exhibits what Economist Friedrich Hayek called "spontaneous order," the emergence of societal order and coordination without central planning. Through the decentralized actions of individuals and businesses pursuing their own interests, a complex web of economic interactions and exchanges emerges, leading to overall societal coordination and prosperity.

Example: In a busy city, people navigate crowded streets, follow traffic rules, and form orderly queues at bus stops or ticket counters—all without the direction of a central authority. Order arises spontaneously as individuals respond to their immediate needs and interact with each other based on social norms and mutual understanding. Similarly, in a free-market system, prices, supply, and demand are coordinated through the interactions of countless market participants, resulting in the efficient allocation of resources and the provision of goods and services in ways that will meet societal needs.

Rule #9

Free agency: Free-market systems allow anyone, within legal limits, to remain in free agency and promote their value to other organizations or start their own organization. Additionally, organizations, within legal limits, can terminate employees who are not providing value or are breaching the rules of employment under organizational standards and policies. Additionally, as employees increase their value to their employers, they can negotiate for increased pay and benefits. Organizations, in turn, can negotiate for greater responsibility, higher levels of performance, and leadership. In free-market systems, free agency is fluid and continuous.

Example: Geoff was a skilled graphic designer whose request for a raise was denied. Disappointed, Geoff applied to various other advertising firms looking for people with his skills. He went on numerous interviews and was offered a few positions. He negotiated his salary and was offered a compensation package 20 percent greater than he was making. He told his employer of the offer and, because his employer didn't want to lose him, offered him a 25 percent increase in total compensation. Geoff and his employer both benefited from his free agency.

Rule #10

Individual responsibility: The most essential rule governing a free-market system is individual responsibility. Without it, the entire system falls apart. When individuals fulfill their obligations and honor commitments, it builds a foundation of trust between buyers and sellers, employers and employees, and business partners. Trust is essential for the smooth functioning of markets, as it allows for transactions and collaborations to take place with confidence. Individual responsibility also encourages personal growth and self-reliance. In a free-market system, individuals are encouraged to take charge of their own economic well-being. They are motivated to acquire new skills, make wise financial decisions, and seek opportunities for growth and advancement. By taking responsibility for their own success, individuals can better navigate the market, adapt to changing circumstances, and overcome challenges.

Example: Mark runs a local restaurant. He is responsible for managing the finances, ensuring the quality of the food, and providing excellent customer service. If he neglects any of these responsibilities, the reputation of his restaurant will suffer, leading to a decline in customers and profits. But if Mark takes individual responsibility seriously, he will make informed decisions, maintain high standards, and actively seek ways to improve his business. The success or failure of Mark's restaurant ultimately rests on his shoulders, highlighting the importance of individual responsibility in driving entrepreneurship, accountability, and the overall functioning of a free-market economic system.

Rules provide a solid foundation for leaders as they develop the disciplines required to think, behave, and communicate in a free-market system and support their efforts to maximize their potential and guide their teams to grow and thrive. Once a leader understands and accept the rules governing free-market systems, they will be prepared to understand and address the next foundation of leadership development: business systems.

Chapter 3 Takeaways

- The free market is where "people" buy, sell, and trade goods and services for an agreed-upon exchange of value with limited government interference.
- Rules are a set of explicit or understood regulations or principles governing conduct within a particular activity or sphere. Understanding the rules of free-market systems empowers leaders to be proactive in the way they think, behave, and communicate.
- Rules provide a solid foundation for leaders as they develop the disciplines required to think, behave, and communicate in a free-market system and support their efforts to maximize their potential and guide their teams to grow and thrive.

CHAPTER 4

Foundation #4

Systems Run Businesses; People Run Systems

Bruce walked into my office disheveled and frustrated. He plopped in a chair, threw his phone on the table, leaned back, and took a deep breath. "I don't know what to do. I have people working for me who don't know what the heck they're doing." He paused for a moment, gathered his thoughts, and continued, "I tell them what to do, make sure they have what they need, then leave. I come back later and they're still not doing it how I told them to. Then I have to fix what they did. I end up doing all the work, so why do I need them?"

As Bruce was talking, his phone began vibrating, he took a quick glance, picked it up, and then tossed it across the floor. He pointed at it and said, "I just finished explaining what I wanted him to do. I told him I had a meeting and not to call me. But he calls anyway. I bet he's already forgotten what I told him." I kept my eyes fixed on Bruce, determined not to say a word until he was done. He rubbed his thumbs on his temples and leaned forward in his chair. "I can't keep doing this. I'm working 80 hours a week and most of the time I'm just fixing people's mistakes. I need people to think for themselves. Maybe I should just sell the business and get out." He took a deep breath and sank back into his chair. His look was one of despair.

Bruce is a second-generation owner of a regional manufacturing company. Over a 20-year period, he has grown his company from $2 million to more than $50 million in revenue. The company has three divisions and more than 150 employees. He has been brilliant at developing innovative solutions to meet clients' needs. He has a relentless drive to succeed and has always looked for opportunities to expand and grow.

Bruce is also beloved by his employees. He is known as a man of high moral character who is kind and willing to help anyone, anytime. But when it came to leadership, he lacked intentionality. He communicated haphazardly, mostly because he spent most of his time in client meetings and most of his attention on bringing in new business. But his employees weren't always sure what was expected of them. He didn't have systems in place for training, onboarding, goal-setting, machine operation, safety, or sales. He lacked processes and procedures for cohesive workflow.

He didn't intend to leave his employees unprepared to succeed, but when leaders do not lead intentionally, they face unintentional consequences.

I looked at Bruce and placed my pen on the table. "Bruce," I started, "let's celebrate your accomplishments. Could you have imagined 20 years ago being where you are today? You've grown your company to 25 times the size it was when you took over. That's extremely rare."

"But you can't lead this company by yourself; you need help. People often joke about wishing they could clone themselves. Well, that's exactly what we're going to do. We're going to clone your thoughts, values, ideas, habits, and systems." I pointed at his phone on the floor and finished my thought. "When we're done, that phone will ring a lot less."

Bruce's circumstances are all too common among business owners, supervisors, and entrepreneurs. He took for granted what he knew and expected others to "get it," then became frustrated when his team couldn't. Bruce had systems. He knew how his business worked; he knew the workflow; he knew where people were supposed to be; he knew how many orders his company had; he knew when and where those orders were to be shipped; he knew his financials inside and out; he knew how to market and sell his products; and he had long-standing relationships with customers. He had systems for all those activities and more, but they were all trapped in his brain. So he had to be involved with every activity, every process, from beginning to end. Which is why his phone rang nonstop, his e-mail inbox was always full, and his stress level was through the roof.

Over the following year, Bruce, a few of his key team members, and I went to work putting systems in place throughout the company. We were very clear about what was to be done and the results that were expected for each area of the business. We wrote everything down in painstaking detail, from sales and marketing to order fulfillment and completion. During the process, we discovered many activities Bruce had been perpetuating that weren't producing the results he wanted. Each time, we adjusted and came up with a better system. Once we wrote everything down, we began to create procedures, training manuals, and key performance indicators (KPIs) for each department. We looked at the hierarchy and began to designate systems responsibilities for each leadership position. We then began training the leaders and team members on the new systems and asked for feedback if they came across something they believed was out of alignment with a process or goal. Once the team was trained, we conducted a leadership development program for the leaders; they emerged empowered to run their departments with clear expectations and systematic feedback.

The following year the company grew its revenue by 15 percent; profitability in its low-margin industry grew by an impressive 7 percent. The department leaders were running Bruce's systems effectively and improving them as needed—and without Bruce's help. Bruce reduced his workweek to 50 hours, was able to spend more time with his family, and even took a vacation.

The daily, weekly, and monthly challenges of Bruce's business continue. If anything, growth has created more challenges. But Bruce now has a team of leaders who take ownership of their divisions. He's no longer alone. Together, they are proving that when leadership is systematic and diverse, there are no limitations on what can be accomplished.

Systems-Based Leadership

Systems run businesses, and people run systems. Systems are a set of things working together within a broader network. Business systems are the processes, procedures, behaviors, strategies, tactics, norms, and communication that are followed to deliver products or services to customers efficiently and effectively. Systems are essential because people spend 95 percent of their time in subconscious habits; our internal mental and emotional processing systems are wired for habituation.

One of the key responsibilities of leaders is to ensure their organization's systems are designed to support their people. Systems play a critical role in shaping habits, which ultimately lead to desired results.

Regardless of their position in the hierarchy, leaders must understand how their business operates from start to finish. In smaller organizations, leaders may oversee multiple departments and systems, while in larger organizations, they might be responsible for the systems of a specific department. Regardless of the scope, it is vital for leaders to understand the inner workings of their entire business, identify their areas of responsibility, analyze the systems that shape their habits, and consistently seek ways to improve those systems to drive better outcomes. *(For an example, see Appendix, Item A: How business systems work in a retail chain and distribution network.)*

Businesses have different levels of systems, an overview system that captures the general workflow across organizational departments, but also systems within departments, more detailed systems that contribute to a cohesive workflow for each of those particular aspects of the operation. By understanding their systems and continuously refining them, leaders can enhance the efficiency and effectiveness of their organization as a whole.

Building detailed systems and helping people understand workflow is hard work. Every step, process, and procedure must be detailed for effective workflow. For every system, there is a person responsible for ensuring the system is followed consistently. And if a person does not understand how to run their systems properly, they will not produce the expected results—and they will slow, stifle, and frustrate other parts of the workflow.

Systems Failures and Toxic Cultures

All too often, in my discussions with business owners, supervisors, and entrepreneurs about their leadership and cultural challenges, I find leaders with toxic cultures assuming the cause is a few bad people who are determined to cause conflict. I'm often asked how they should manage the conflict. I'm often met with puzzled looks when I tell them that before we discuss conflict management, they need to take our business health assessment, which will reveal how intentional they are in their systems. Nearly all culture and conflict issues are the result of systems failures.

Our greatest intrinsic motivation is to belong and contribute to a purpose bigger than ourselves. Most people are not taught or encouraged to think systematically and most organizations do not teach their employees how and why their systems work. I've spoken to hundreds of employees in toxic cultures who are frustrated because their leaders do not teach or empower them to be responsible for the systems they are running. Most employees are hungry to contribute at higher levels, but most leaders do not write their systems down, teach people what they are responsible for, or empower them to own their responsibility for ensuring those systems run effectively.

As a result, employees lack trust in their organizations and organizations fail to capitalize on their employees' potential. Employees often believe that their leaders don't share what they know because passing along their knowledge will make them less valuable to the company. Of course, the opposite is true; leaders increase their value by increasing the value of those they lead. By teaching and empowering their employees with systems-based thinking, they can produce at higher levels and increase their organizations' efficiency and profitability. Bill Vaughan once said, "You only keep what you give away."[1] Leaders must teach their systems and allow their employees to own their responsibilities. That is not only an effective way to run a business, it is the most effective way to clone new leaders.

More often than not, the root of toxic cultures is systems failures that do not allow employees to do their best work. They become frustrated, and when they are frustrated over prolonged periods of time, they can become hostile toward others. If leaders focus on ensuring their systems are clear, they empower their employees to run them. In such an environment, selfish, manipulative, and disagreeable employees will be exposed, and then you can use conflict management strategies to help them shape up or ship out.

Systems Thinking

Systems thinking requires leaders to think first on a macroscale, then identify how the micro affects the macro. Most businesses have sales and marketing, operations, finance and administration, culture and human resources, and executive leadership groups or departments. Executive leadership must be clear about the responsibilities, systems, and expected results of those they place in leadership positions in those departments and divisions. Then it is those leaders' jobs to evaluate their systems, ensure the systems are conducive to the expected results, and be responsible for leading the people in their departments who operate the systems.

The question for every leader is, "Are your systems creating habits that lead to the results you want?" If not, it's time to consider changing, adjusting, or overhauling the systems so new habits can be formed.

The appendix for this chapter includes a list of evaluation questions covering two distinct leadership oversight areas: organizational systems and roles and responsibilities. Leaders must understand and have oversight of these systems if they want to put people in the best positions to succeed. Leaders do not need to know all the details in each area, but they need to be well connected with the people who are. The only way leaders can manage systems well is through consistent evaluation. The questions in the appendix will serve as a starting point to gather feedback from employees regarding the organization's systems and roles and responsibilities. By encouraging open and honest communication leaders open up more opportunities for creative ideas and ownership. It is true teambuilding when groups of people discuss how to improve the business they all contribute to, then decide to change together. I encourage every leader to use the appendix questions to start the process. Then they can customize their own. The important thing is to get started.

One last note for this section: It is vital that leaders do not become defensive when listening to their employees. As my friend Dale Karmie[2] says, "Big toes get stepped on." Leaders cannot take offense to feedback. Rather, they need to think systematically about how the feedback can help them improve their systems so they can put their employees in the best position to succeed.

People Can Change With Systems Changes

Some leaders believe that even if systems change, people won't. But people don't lose their ability to change and grow. No organization needs to be stuck doing the same things over and over and expecting different results. Instead, they can evaluate their systems, change them, lead their people toward better habits, and enjoy better outcomes.

Again, a business leader's job can be stated simply: Put your people in the best position to succeed, then empower them to succeed on their own. Leaders cannot put people in the best position to succeed unless they first understand how their business runs and the systems that run it. And leaders cannot run their businesses effectively if they do not have systems in place to empower people to run systems on their own. If leaders are not intentional about building effective systems, they cannot consistently lead to high performance, no matter how excellent their interpersonal relationship skills are. Nor will they attract or retain high performers who want to be a part of high-performing organizations.

There are too many leadership development programs that teach leaders to appease people. But people are most happy when they are most productive, and they are most productive when systems are well defined and well communicated, and each person knows their responsibilities and what is expected of them. Most of the time when things are not working in a business, it's a systems problem. And most of the time when things go wrong, people blame others, complain about something out of their control, or make excuses. That rarely happens at organizations that are clear about their systems and empower their people to run them effectively.

Once systems are well established and systems-based thinking is implemented, leaders can focus on guiding, mentoring, coaching, teaching, and admonishing their employees to reach their full potential. To do so, leaders must understand the foundations of human motivation.

Chapter 4 Takeaways

- Systems are a set of things working together within a broader network. Business systems are the processes, procedures, behaviors, strategies, tactics, norms, and communication that are followed to deliver products or services to customers efficiently and effectively.
- Systems play a critical role in shaping habits, which ultimately lead to desired results.
- If leaders focus on ensuring their systems are clear, they empower their employees to run them.

- It is vital for leaders to understand the inner workings of their entire business, identify their areas of responsibility, analyze the systems that shape their habits, and consistently seek ways to improve those systems to drive better outcomes.
- Leaders increase their value by increasing the value of those they lead.
- A business leader's job can be stated simply: Put your people in the best position to succeed, then empower them to succeed on their own.
- If leaders are not intentional about building effective systems, they cannot consistently lead to high performance, no matter how excellent their interpersonal relationship skills.

CHAPTER 5

Foundation #5

The PVD System and Channeling Human Motivation

Years ago, my consultancy was engaged by a manufacturing company to help them identify, develop, and coach their next-generation leaders. Their CEO and executive leadership team were closing in on retirement, and they wanted to ensure the company would be sustainable in their absence. The executives came up with a list of young men and women in the organization who they felt had the greatest leadership potential. My team and I went to work conducting assessments and analyzing which of the young leaders had the greatest potential based on their assessment scores.

One of the people on the list was a young man, let's call him "Troy." Among the candidates, he scored the highest in leadership potential. I highlighted his name and shared it with the executive team. One of the executives commented that although Troy was intelligent, competent, and proficient in relationships, he lacked passion; he wondered if Troy had the drive and desire to lead. They approached Troy about enrolling in our program, and he agreed, though not enthusiastically.

The leadership program was comprehensive and consisted of training on the systems of the organization, the leadership responsibilities, best leadership practices, the industry, and the compensation a leadership position provided. The program also included individual coaching and mentorship sessions to help participants clarify how their goals and vision aligned with the organization's. The company invested a significant amount of time, money, and other resources in the program; in exchange, they asked the candidates to participate in the coaching and mentorship sessions on their own time to show their commitment to their personal development. The participants agreed, and we went to work.

As I began working with Troy, it was easy to see his potential, but it was also easy to recognize his lack of motivation. He was doing everything required of him: showed up to his sessions, fulfilled his obligations, participated in discussions, and completed all assignments on time and with proficiency. But something was missing.

During that time, I was coaching my son's Little League Baseball team, and one afternoon we happened to be playing Troy's son's team. Troy was the head coach, and before, during, and after the game, I was mesmerized as I observed his passion, excitement, communication skills, care, and energy on full display. It was amazing to see how those youngsters responded to him; they played with an incredible amount of excitement and passion.

In my next session with Troy, I pointed out how much different he was on the baseball diamond than at the company. He told me, "I grew up without my dad, and a lot of those kids on my team don't have a dad in their lives, so I feel like it's my job to be the dad they don't have when they're with me." I asked him what he thought made a good dad, and he listed many things such as instilling confidence, helping them overcome adversity, teaching them the right way to do things, being there for them no matter what, and helping them correct their mistakes.

I went on to ask him if he ever considered transferring the idea of being a good dad into his company leadership. He told me he hadn't thought of it that way. I went on to tell him that many of the people he would lead at the organization also grew up without their fathers, and just like his baseball players, many employees at the company needed someone to help them gain confidence and overcome adversity, to teach them the right way to do their jobs, be there for them no matter what, and give the guidance they need to correct their mistakes. Troy's eyes lit up; his passion was noticeable.

We talked about what it would look like to lead his team at work like he led his baseball team. At the end of our session, Troy was excited, and he committed to engaging in a new way from then on. And he did. Over the following months of our program, Troy was the most lively, engaged, and inspirational person in our cohort. His passion was infectious, and many of the other participants' passion increased as well. Troy was promoted to shift supervisor and is leading dozens of people who are performing at the highest levels.

Troy had the passion all along; he simply lacked the connection to a greater purpose to draw it out. Once he connected the dots, he simply channeled his purpose into leadership.

Understanding Human Motivation

The concept of motivation refers to the inner drive or reason that compels someone to act or behave in a certain way. Behavioral scientists, psychologists, and social researchers have spent years studying the factors that contribute to human motivation and fulfillment. Countless studies have been conducted cross-culturally in an effort to reduce the impact of variables such as environment, belief systems, and economic status.

Many of the findings were included in a fascinating documentary, *Happy*,[1] which reported on years of research on the factors that contributed to making people happy. The documentarians first interviewed and surveyed people from all walks of life on what they believed would make them happy. Then they spent time studying, interviewing, and surveying people who claimed to be happy. They then broke the responses into two categories: extrinsic motivators, what people believed would make them happy, and intrinsic motivators, what made people happy. The responses for each are as follows.

Extrinsic Motivators

1. Money
2. Fame
3. Power

Intrinsic Motivators

1. Being connected in relationships.
2. Making personal progress toward worthwhile goals.
3. Belonging and contributing to a purpose bigger than self.

Extrinsic Motivators

Further studies on extrinsic motivators yield interesting discoveries. People who *attained* money, fame, or power through focused pursuit did not report increases in happiness. Many reported increased feelings of depression, delusion, and anxiety. They later discovered that what brought them happiness was the *pursuit* of money, fame, or power. Attaining them provided short-lived feelings of happiness followed by sadness that the pursuit was over. They then felt anxious about the future. Many reasoned they had dreamed too small and set higher goals for more money, fame, or power. Others adjusted their pursuits to find happiness in other ways, which led to spiritual journeys, career changes, and philanthropy.

In the study,[2] by Matthew A. Killingsworth, Daniel Kahneman, and Barbara Mellers, conducted in 2022, money, the greatest extrinsic motivator, did not produce increases in happiness after a person reached the compensation threshold of $75,000 per year. People with families making less than $75,000 per year found it difficult to meet basic needs, which increased anxiety and decreased happiness. But the study showed little to no neurological difference in happiness levels between a person who made $75,000 per year and $500,000 per year.

As to fame and power, the findings of the study were generally the same. Upon attaining them, people felt anxious. Their focus then shifted from attaining to maintaining fame and power. For many, the focus on maintaining fame or power dimmed their passion and sapped their energy for further pursuit. Also similar to the pursuit of money, people either set higher goals for greater positions of fame and power or they looked elsewhere for happiness.

Intrinsic Motivators

Further studies on intrinsic motivators also produced fascinating discoveries. Seven different studies revealed that connection in relationships predicted better health and longer lifespans. They also established that positive feelings associated with connection make people more creative and resilient. Furthermore, neurobiologists have demonstrated that connection increases oxytocin, the hormone associated with trust, whereas when people feel disconnected, the body increases cortisol, the "fight or flight" hormone. Sustained elevation in cortisol levels increases anxiety and impairs memory. Connection also improves affinity and trust for an organization.[3]

Studies show that people have much higher levels of emotional and mental well-being as they make progress toward worthwhile goals. Feeling that goals were attainable was more important to study participants than attaining the goal itself. Additionally, the *Neuroscience of Goals and Behavior Change* study[4] showed no difference in well-being relative to age. Participants—the survey included participants ages 18 to 92—reported that setting clear, worthwhile goals helped them feel in control of their lives, which gave them direction for their actions. This helped them relax and stay focused on important tasks, which led to greater feelings of happiness.

Scientific research shows that belonging and contributing to a purpose bigger than self is a powerful pathway to personal growth and lasting happiness. Magnetic resonance imaging (MRI) data show that giving altruistically activates the same parts of the brain stimulated by food and sex. Experiments demonstrate that giving is hardwired in the brain—and it's pleasurable. Helping others has been linked to helping people live lives that are not only happier but healthier, wealthier, more productive, and meaningful.

The primary focus of most business leaders and organizations is extrinsic—making more money, cutting costs, avoiding taxes, avoiding lawsuits, finding new opportunities to do business, and finding inexpensive ways to fund business growth. Every one of these responsibilities is vital for the growth and sustainability of a business. But the majority of these responsibilities are centered on extrinsic motivations, things that can be attained, not things that can be given. Without an intentional focus on things such as leadership and personal development, empowerment, and scaling, a business cannot sustain.

Extrinsic motivators are good, important, and must be a major consideration for effective leadership. Too often, people view the extrinsic motivators of money, fame, and power in a silo and conclude that human beings are greedy and selfish and want to control others. But if viewed from a logical, gracious, and practical perspective, it's easy to understand their value and importance.

> *Money*: People need money to take care of their fundamental needs: shelter, food, utilities, and transportation. The desire for money is universal, and when people work, they want to be fairly compensated for the value they provide to their organization. Money is also important for business stability, growth, and sustainability. But how a business makes money determines how much it will make and how long it can be sustained.
>
> *Fame*: People want to be recognized, appreciated, and valued for their work. No one wants to live an obscure life without impact. We all desire to make an impact, and therefore, being recognized and pseudo-famous within our organizations is a positive motivation.
>
> *Power*: People want to know they have a say in their lives. To give up your power means you're not free to make your own choices or to come and go as you please. Without a sense of power, we can become powerless, and powerlessness breeds despair, depression, and fear.

Extrinsic motivations are important, but they lose some of their luster upon the attainment of money, fame, or power. Therefore, to sustain organizational motivation, leaders must channel extrinsic through intrinsic motivation. To demonstrate how this can be done effectively and sustainably, we will need to recall much of what we've discussed in our earlier chapters and channel it through the PVD System.

The PVD System

As we have stated, systems run businesses, and people run systems. In an organization, there are systems for workflow and for the way we think, behave, and communicate as a culture. The PVD system—purpose, vision, and disciplines—helps leaders create clarity around the people systems designed to create better habits and mechanisms for higher achievement.

Purpose in the PVD system is about discovering your unique strengths, competencies, and passions for your organization and yourself. Vision refers to clarity of direction. It is direction, not intention that leads to a destination. You cannot lead if you're not sure where you're going.

Disciplines inform habits. Either you create and have intentional outcomes or you will have to accept unintentional consequences.

It is vital that leaders never forget that people live 95 percent of their lives in subconscious habits. The PVD system helps leaders become intentionally habitual in channeling extrinsic circumstances through intrinsic thinking, behaving, and communication process that leads to better decisions and better, holistic outcomes.

Purpose

The entire human experience is a journey to define and justify purpose. Unfortunately, most people feel they are without purpose. In fact, according to research,[5] 57 percent of people say they don't know their purpose, which leads to purposeless behaviors, depression, anxiety, and carelessness.

Purpose refers to the reason something is done, created, or exists. Purpose includes discovering a "why," but it always starts with "who."

Mankind's greatest intrinsic motivation is to belong and contribute to a purpose bigger than self. And according to countless studies, philosophical debates, and human experience, the greatest purpose of humankind is to help other humans live better lives.

High-performing leaders, business owners, middle managers, and entrepreneurs are clear about "who" they help and "how" they help them have a better life holistically. And when they are able to clearly communicate and mobilize their teams toward a greater purpose, they help each team member live from a purpose and with a purpose.

Business owners often underestimate their purpose. A manufacturer might believe that they only create parts for aerospace, rail, auto, or heavy equipment. A health care provider might believe they only work on a certain part of the human body, failing to understand their holistic effect on a patient's life. Financial service providers may believe they only manage portfolios or do tax and audit compliance, failing to appreciate how important their work is to protecting the future of a business. The things people do often don't explain the purpose of their business or why their business exists.

When viewed from a perspective of purpose, the work people do becomes much more important. Manufacturers make parts that help people travel safer, provide for their families, create experiences with loved ones, and further their careers. Health care providers ensure that our physiological health is at its peak so we can experience life to its full measure. Financial service providers help people provide security for their loved ones, ensure their futures, and preserve their families' legacies. This understanding, focus, and intentionality toward a deeper purpose ignite passion, creativity, and intrinsic motivation that leads to greater fulfillment—and to greater extrinsic rewards such as money, fame, and empowerment.

I often ask business leaders to share client testimonials. Their eyes light up as they tell me stories of clients who have told them how the solutions they provided alleviated their stress, made them look good to their clients, helped them advance in their business, or created new opportunities. A client rarely talks about a solution itself but about how the solution has improved the quality of their life.

To spark and maintain motivation, leaders must clearly communicate how their organization is intentional about helping their team understand how they contribute to a purpose that positively affects humankind, how they provide connection and belonging, and how their purpose helps their team members and clients become the best of who they are.

Intrinsic motivation is a source of energy that never runs out. The more a person lives from intrinsic motivation, the more their motivation grows, which leads to greater extrinsic rewards. However, many of my clients have reported that as they gain more extrinsic rewards, the less they care about them and the more focused they become on their purpose. Additionally, living from a purpose helps leaders become more intentional because the purpose is as important to minor decisions as it is to major decisions.

One of my clients, let's call him Craig, owns a surfacing company. When we began our relationship, Craig was unclear about his organization's purpose. For years, he was struggling to stay above breakeven and had considered liquidating his business and going to work for someone else. So, we spent time discovering his purpose. We became clear about whom he helped, how he helped them have a better quality of life, why that mattered, and how to be intentional with every decision toward that purpose. We put mechanisms in place for Craig to track extrinsic factors, such as revenue and profit. Specifically, we built his growth strategy around how to create more client testimonials. To do this, we discussed the purpose behind every activity, from the way his team did consultations to the way they scheduled jobs to the way they handled customer service and the way they dressed, behaved, and communicated.

Over time, purpose-thinking became a habit for Craig and his team. Continuous improvement in their business systems was the new norm, which led to greater client satisfaction, which led to more of the best kind of advertising, word-of-mouth advertising. Craig's organization grew by more than 300 percent, and he now has three locations and three full-time crews, as well as greater feelings of personal fulfillment and less stress.

Purpose is not an esoteric ideal; it is practical. *(For a list of questions leaders can use to discover their organization's purpose and how they can employ purpose to get their team in the best position to succeed, see Appendix, Item B.)*

Vision

When leaders are clear about their organization's purpose, they have the foundation for clearly communicating how each team member's purpose contributes to the organization's purpose. However, to put everyone in the best position to succeed, leaders must be clear about the "V" in the PVD system, vision.

According to Brian Tracy,[6] "A genius without a roadmap is lost in any country." If leaders are unsure where they want to go or unsure about how to get to where they want to go, they are lost. When people are lost, the most common emotions are frustration, fear, despair, and hopelessness. According to *Harvard Business Review*,[7] 97 percent of organizations do not operate with a clear vision.

When clients engage in my organization for a consultation, they are usually struggling with cultural challenges that are leading to poor performance. One of the first questions we ask them is, "What is your vision?"

Often, they either don't know or don't have one. This is understandable, as it is so easy to become habitually reactive in the midst of daily demands and expectations. However, a lack of vision creates frustration, fear, despair, and hopelessness in organizations and causes burnout for leaders who feel they are on a metaphoric hamster wheel and not achieving the results they want.

One of the leading three intrinsic motivators is "making personal progress towards worthwhile goals." Without a clear vision, individual goals are relegated to simple tasks that don't allow people to see the broader picture of how they belong and contribute to a purpose bigger than self. An organization could have a great purpose, but it is direction, not intention, that leads to the destination. For a purpose to be fulfilled, it must be filtered through a clear and compelling vision.

In our vision-casting workshops, we begin by breaking participants into small groups, giving each group a 50-piece puzzle and asking them to familiarize themselves with the puzzle picture on the box. We then designate a "leader" of the group, give them the box with the picture, and instruct them not to share the picture with the rest of their group while they work on the puzzle. To create urgency and encourage focus, we set a time limit for completing the puzzle. Then we start the timer. When they get stuck, the leader reminds them of what the picture looks like and guides them in placing the pieces in their proper place. To this day, we have never had a group complete the puzzle in the allotted time on their first attempt.

As they try, we typically see a mix of uncertainty, confusion, miscommunication, mistakes, laughter, frustration, and learning. After the first attempt, we allow the entire group to look at the picture again, discuss what worked and what didn't, and then we repeat the cycle until they complete the exercise within the allotted time. In each attempt, the group grows more confident, competitive, and competent. And when the group finally accomplishes the task, there is a joyful celebration, even among the most polished professionals.

Afterwards, we debrief and ask the participants what they thought the rationale of the exercise was, that is, what they learned from it. We receive a variety of answers, such as the importance of communication, patience, and knowing your role and responsibility. But the most common answer is the importance of remembering what the picture looks like.

Vision is a clear mental picture of the future as it should be, compelled by the conviction that it should be. Conviction is a deeply held belief that an organization's purpose is to improve the quality of life for humankind. I can't overemphasize the importance of conviction in an organization's vision. As noted in Chapter 1, there are three certainties in life—pain, uncertainty, and the need for constant work. To create a clear and compelling vision, leaders must look to the future and decide how they will reduce pain and uncertainty and make work fulfilling and meaningful.

Purpose precedes vision and vision perpetuates purpose. Leaders can create a clear vision without a purpose rooted in intrinsic motivation, but it will not be compelling. Again, the greatest intrinsic motivation is to belong and contribute to a purpose bigger than self. Fulfilling a purpose and vision is one of the most challenging undertakings in life; if it is not a compelling journey, people will not fight through the pain, uncertainty, and constant work it requires.

When casting vision, it is important for leaders to look as far into the future as possible: 3, 5, 10, and 20 years. But it is difficult for the human mind, body, and spirit to align actionable disciplines with vision unless it is presented in one-year increments; think of vision casting as a funnel with a broad range at the top and narrow at the bottom. As well, a vision should start holistically and then be broken into categories for each department and division and subsequently within each department and division. *(For a vision-casting Q&A exercise for leaders, see Appendix, Item C.)*

Consider the following one-year business vision broken down into departmental categories:

- Sales and Marketing:
  - Increase sales revenue by 20 percent through a targeted marketing campaign and improve customer retention strategies.

- Expand market reach by entering two new geographic regions and securing strategic partnerships with complementary businesses.
- Enhance brand visibility and customer engagement through a robust social media presence and content marketing initiatives.

- Operations:
  - Optimize operational efficiency by implementing lean principles and process improvements to achieve a 15 percent reduction in production costs.
  - Streamline supply chain management through the adoption of a new inventory management system, reducing stock outs and improving order fulfillment speed.
  - Improve customer satisfaction by implementing a customer relationship management (CRM) system to enhance communication and provide personalized experiences.
- Finance and Administration:
  - Achieve a 10 percent increase in profitability through cost control measures and revenue optimization.
  - Implement a cloud-based accounting system to streamline financial processes, improve accuracy, and provide real-time reporting.
  - Conduct a thorough financial analysis to identify potential areas for cost savings and investment opportunities.
- Culture and Human Resources:
  - Foster a culture of continuous learning and development by implementing a training and mentorship program for employees.
  - Enhance employee engagement by introducing flexible work arrangements and wellness initiatives.
  - Improve communication and collaboration by implementing regular team-building activities and open-door policies.
- Executive Leadership:
  - Provide strategic guidance and support to departments, aligning their efforts with the overall vision and goals.

- ○ Establish key performance indicators (KPIs) and implement a system for tracking and monitoring progress.
- ○ Cultivate a culture of innovation and adaptability by encouraging experimentation and embracing new technologies.

Once you have completed your vision for each department, conduct the same exercises within each department.

As leaders review the specifics of the vision for their business and each company department, they begin to recognize the importance of thinking holistically about their organization, regardless of their position. Every leader must be able to understand and clearly communicate how their department, division, and responsibilities affect the organization's overall vision. Again, too many leadership development programs are focused solely on helping leaders gain interpersonal skills, but leadership in context means being out front, leading the way, guiding the journey, and that is impossible to do without a clear and compelling vision. Casting a clear and compelling vision is extraordinary. It flies in the face of the status quo and will separate organizations from their competitors.

Disciplines

I am your constant companion. I am your greatest helper or heaviest burden. I will push you onward or drag you down to failure. I am completely at your command. Half of the things you do, you might as well turn over to me, and I will be able to do them quickly and correctly. I am easily managed, but you must be firm with me. Show me exactly how you want something done, and after a few lessons, I will do it automatically. I am the servant of all great leaders and, alas, of all failures as well.

I am *HABIT*.

It is worth repeating: Human beings live 95 percent of their lives in subconscious habit. Disciplines inform habits.

Part 1 of *The Leadership Edge* has been devoted to providing leaders with a foundation for putting their organization, division, department, and team in the best position to succeed. After reading and completing the exercises, leaders will know the seven elements required to develop as a strong leader. They will understand what leadership is and the purpose and vision behind it. They will understand the free-market system and how systems run businesses and people run systems. They will have a firm grasp on intrinsic and extrinsic motivations. And they will be able to channel their knowledge and understanding through purpose and into a clear and compelling vision.

But without discipline, none of that matters. I have a picture on my wall that includes the words: "Ideas without execution are useless." It is a constant reminder that unless I discipline myself in action toward fulfilling my purpose and vision, I will fall short. Just as if someone created a financial plan for their family, complete with purpose, vision, and actions, but did not discipline themselves to follow it. Their purpose and vision would amount to nothing. The same will be true for leaders who create plans and do not discipline themselves to see them through.

Part 2 of *The Leadership Edge* is dedicated to leadership disciplines. Leaders will be provided with specific tools to effectively lead themselves, others, and teams in real time toward fulfilling their organization's and their own purpose and vision.

Before leaving Part 1, I want to emphasize that the foundations of leadership development must be revisited and strengthened. Everything that sustains has a great foundation. If a building is lost to a catastrophe, as long as there is a solid foundation, it can be rebuilt. Leaders can never forget or neglect the foundations of leadership.

Chapter 5 Takeaways

- Scientific research shows that belonging and contributing to a purpose bigger than self is a powerful pathway to personal growth and lasting happiness.
- The PVD system—purpose, vision, and discipline—helps leaders create clarity around the people systems designed to create better habits and mechanisms for higher achievement.
- Mankind's greatest intrinsic motivation is to belong and contribute to a purpose bigger than self.
- Intrinsic motivation is a source of energy that never runs out. The more a person lives from intrinsic motivation, the

more their motivation grows, which leads to greater extrinsic rewards.

- Purpose in the PVD system is about discovering your unique strengths, competencies, and passions for your organization and yourself.
- Vision is a clear mental picture of the future as it should be, compelled by the conviction that it should be.
- Human beings live 95 percent of their lives in subconscious habit. Disciplines inform habits.

PART 2

Leadership Development Disciplines

CHAPTER 6

Personal Responsibility and PVD

Self-leadership, it starts within,
A sacred place where dreams begin,
To know thyself, with honesty embrace,
The strengths, the flaws, the depths, the grace.

For when we wander, lost and astray,
Or fight adversities that stand in our way,
It is within ourselves we find the light,
To steer our ship through darkest night.

No captain sails without a vision clear,
No conductor guides without a listening ear,
To lead oneself, one must learn,
To guide and direct their soul that yearns

In solitude's embrace, we find our might,
To conquer fears and scale the height,
To chart our course, our destiny create,
With self-belief, our doubts abate.

In every choice, a chance to lead,
To plant the seeds of a noble creed,
To take responsibility, bold and true,
For actions that shape the world we view.

For leaders rise, not just in name,
But in deeds, purpose their flame,

They inspire hearts with integrity strong,
Empowering others to rise along.

So heed the call within your soul,
Embrace self-leadership, let it unfold,
For in this dance of life, you"ll find,
The strength to lead and leave behind
A legacy of truth, love, and art,
A life well-lived, a leader's heart.

—Author Unknown

The 20th-century American entrepreneur and motivational speaker John Earl Shoaff liked to say, "Work harder on yourself than you do on your job. Working on your job will earn you a living, but working on yourself will earn you a fortune."

Self-leadership is the most important, challenging, and rewarding leadership discipline of all. Someone sufficiently disciplined to lead the person they look at in the mirror will have what it takes to lead others. Self-leadership requires a person to look deep within themselves and discover their gifts, strengths, weaknesses, and identity. It requires acceptance, self-guidance, and admonishment. It is a brave and trying path, but having achieved the discipline, a self-leader will have the capacity, strength, and efficacy to lead others. Having mastered themselves, self-leaders are able to put others in a position to succeed. It is hardly counterintuitive; it resoundingly fulfills the old adage, "to change the world, you must start with yourself."

I often see leaders using shame to try to motivate themselves toward greater self-leadership. I remind them that the substance they use to motivate themselves toward change is the substance they'll rely on to sustain it. Renowned shame researcher Brene Brown defines the difference between guilt and shame as "I have done something wrong" versus "I am something wrong."

People are professional mistake-makers. On the journey to becoming a better leader, people will make countless mistakes. I encourage them to look at mistakes as feedback, not as an indication that they do not have what it takes to be a leader or that there is something wrong with them.

The disciplines of thinking, behaving, and communicating as an effective leader can be learned and mastered, but the journey is one of many mistakes. And shame cannot be what drives you. Instead, I encourage leaders to think about how their leadership will positively affect their lives and the lives of those they lead. If that is the focus, the process will be more enjoyable and their leadership skills sustainable.

The Power of Personal Responsibility

In a free-market system, we are all, regardless of tax filing status, business owners. This is not a platitude or a motivational idea to get you to think beyond your title; it is fact. In Chapter 3, we discussed the rules of a free-market economic system, such as free agency, competition, consumer sovereignty, and voluntary exchange. The rules apply just as much to individuals as to corporations. Every person entering the marketplace is a business entity, and their value is based on their technical skills, knowledge, character, communication and negotiation skills, relationships, ingenuity, work ethic, perseverance, and trustworthiness. Their market value is predicated not only on their skill level but also on their ability to use those skills to solve problems and produce results. Their pay scale is based on the value they bring to their clients. If that "business entity" wants to earn more, it can do one of two things: increase its skills and focus on higher-value solutions for its clients, or duplicate its skills in others and scale its ability to provide more client solutions.

To multiply their value at an even higher scale, they can do the two simultaneously. Those in leadership positions make more money because it is expected that they will increase their skills and duplicate their skills in others, creating more value for their clients, and by association, organization.

Regardless of their title, position, or financial status, a nonownership leader's "employer" should not be thought of as an employer but as their largest client. I ask my clients if they've made money anywhere else than from their organization in the past few years. The answer is usually yes. I make the point that they have more than one client and inform them that in a free-market system, they can have as many clients as they want and that their employment agreement is actually a client/vendor contract or an open purchase order that is on auto-renew. This usually leads to comments, discussions, and questions on a variety of things, such as negotiations, legalese, tax compliance, and compensation. But it always leads to the same conclusion: Everyone in a free-market system is a business owner and everyone is responsible for the choices they make, the value they bring to the marketplace, increasing their value, having a positive attitude, giving their best effort, and fostering cooperation. Too often people respond with, "I'm working for the man," or "I just work to pay the bills," or "I just do what I have to do to get by." These are powerless and unfortunate ways of viewing work.

But when people understand and accept that in the marketplace they are a business entity, it changes the way they view themselves and their "employer." It gives them a powerful mindset of responsibility and allows them to look at their organization holistically. It also changes how they lead. If you look at everyone on your team as a business owner partnering with you and you are the leader of the partnership (versus the "boss") trying to pull everyone along, your focus will shift to how you can put your partners in the best position to succeed. You will focus on their overall contribution—and on how their efforts lead to compensation increases.

The most effective leaders, regardless of their level, have a very high standard of personal responsibility. They do not partake in or condone BCDE: blame, complaining, deflection, and excuses. The BCDE are poisons people use to shirk responsibility. They destroy teams and organizations. Effective leaders focus on what they can control, and in life, there are only three things you can control: your own attitude, your own effort, and your own level of cooperation.

The first five words of Dr. Joseph Rost's definition of leadership (see Chapter 2, p. __) are, "Leadership is an influence relationship." We cannot control others. We cannot control outcomes. We cannot control vendors, clients, or the government. We can, however, influence others' attitudes, efforts, and cooperation through our own attitudes, efforts, and cooperation.

Furthermore, everyone has a choice. If leadership is not putting them in the best position to succeed, is haphazard in the way they operate, is not clear with expectations, and treats them poorly, that person has the option—Shall we say "duty"?—to confront leadership and negotiate change. And if the organization refuses to change, they have the power of free agency. They can leave and work somewhere else.

When I work with organizations experiencing cultural challenges, and I explain the power of personal responsibility and free agency, I am often met with BCDE. I reply, "You do not have to like the rules of a free-market system, but they are the rules; you can accept or reject them." Accepting means taking personal responsibility for attitude, effort, and cooperation. Rejecting them means giving up your power and allowing someone else to dictate the trajectory of your life.

When every individual in an organization decides to control what they can control and focuses on leading themselves well and influencing others to the best of their ability, the results are remarkable—not just in terms of monetary gains, but greater personal fulfillment, less anxiety, greater commitment, and deep relationships. On the other hand, I have seen the devastating effects on organizations where people don't take personal responsibility and refuse to take control of what they can control, and it leads to high turnover, shrinking revenues, in-fighting, coercion, manipulation, and, ultimately, demise.

In a free-market system, we all have the choice to accept or reject the power of personal responsibility. But make no mistake; you cannot be an effective leader without taking it on.

Your Personal PVD

In Chapter 5, we discussed the PVD system (purpose, vision, and disciplines), which "allows leaders the opportunity to create clarity around the people systems designed to create better habits and mechanisms for higher achievement." We addressed PVD from an organizational perspective. But as you think of yourself as a business entity, it is important to discover your own PVD.

Remember our premise that the highest purpose of humankind is to improve the quality of people's lives. Therefore, you must personally discover how your skills, competencies, and passions improve the quality of other people's lives. Vision is about direction and deciding how you want to use your purpose to improve as many lives as possible. This requires mapping out the activities, disciplines, and outcomes you envision.

Discipline starts with values. Values are no-compromise behaviors that guide us and that keep us consistent in what we do to put ourselves in a position to achieve the outcomes we desire. To guide you in this process, here are questions that you will need to consider, write down, and share with a peer or mentor who can hold you accountable as you move forward.

- *Purpose:* To help individuals discover their purpose, I often use Ikigai, a Japanese concept encapsulating the essence of a fulfilling life. It is a convergence of four elements: what you are passionate about, what you are good at, what the world needs, and what you can get paid to do. The goal is to find the perfect balance where passion, talents, purpose, and profession intersect. It represents a deep sense of purpose and contentment, leading to greater happiness and overall well-being.

Some questions to guide you in this process:

- Natural strengths: What are your natural strengths? *(See Appendix, Item D for answers to help you develop your own list.)*
- Learned skills: What skills have you learned or mastered through education, practice, and experience? List as many as possible. *(See Appendix, Item E for examples.)*
  After you've composed your list of natural strengths and skills, review your lists and decide which strengths and skills you are most passionate about. Rank each on a sliding scale from 1 to 5: 1—Least Passionate, 2—Less Passionate, 3—Somewhat Passionate, 4—More Passionate, 5—Most Passionate. Then create a written list of your skills and strengths using the sliding scale.
- What you get paid to do: What skills, natural strengths, and things you are passionate about do you get paid to do? List as many as possible, then apply the percentage of your time you spend on each. For example, see Figure 6.1.
  At first, the percentages you assign will be arbitrary, but what's important is that you become intentional about putting yourself in a position to use your strengths, passions, and

Skill	Passion Scale	Percentage of my pay
Data Analytics	5	15%
Customer service	2	50%
Managing software	4	15%
Researching client information	3	15%
Financial management	5	5%

Figure 6.1 Skills, Passion, and Pay Scale

skills to solve more problems. This will lead to greater and more sustainable financial gain, increased energy, and greater focus.

Being more purpose-focused in your work does not happen overnight. You must make small incremental changes over time. You don't want to abruptly quit working in the areas that get you paid before you have replaced that income with your Ikigai. The ultimate goal is to work 70 percent of your time in Ikigai.

Ikigai can also be used to encourage team cohesiveness. I recommend having your team go through this exercise with the work that you are currently doing. Assess your team's strengths, passions, and skills, and see if adjustments can be made to put people in a better position to work in their Ikigai. So often, because people live in perpetual habit, they fail to take the time to evaluate their team in the context of skills, strengths, and passions. A little adjustment in position could make all the difference between high and low performance.

- *Vision:* Intentional simply means living from a purpose and with a purpose. Vision is about living with a purpose and being intentional in everything you do to reach a desired destination.

If you are in Cleveland, Ohio, and your intention is to get to Tampa, Florida, but your direction is taking you to Denver, Colorado, no matter how great your purpose for getting to Tampa is, if you keep going in the same direction, you will end up in Denver.

In graduate school, I conducted a survey in which I asked 300 people from different walks of life to share their personal vision. Ninety-three percent answered, "I do not know" or "I do not have one." That was appalling and one of many reasons I dedicated myself to helping people become intentional in self-leadership. We all understand how short life is. In her 2011 book *The Top Five Regrets of the Dying*, palliative nurse Bronnie Ware reported that the biggest regret was voiced as, "I wish I'd had the courage to live a life true to myself, not the life others expected of me."

Determining your vision and acting according to it takes courage. You will have to venture to places you don't know, meet people you haven't met, take risks you've never taken, and stretch yourself in mind, body, and spirit. But it is in pursuit of a worthwhile vision where people feel most alive. According to Dr. Andrew Huberman, when a person is in the pursuit of a worthwhile vision, they experience increased releases of the neurotransmitters dopamine, serotonin, and oxytocin into their central nervous system. Dopamine boosts motivation, learning, and pleasure, fueling drive and reinforcing positive behaviors. Serotonin enhances mood, emotional well-being, sleep, and appetite control. Oxytocin fosters social bonding, trust, and stress reduction. These neurotransmitters contribute to overall well-being, happiness, and positive interpersonal relationships.

Those without a vision reported lower levels of those neurotransmitters and higher levels of cortisol, the stress hormone. The ancient proverb, "Without vision people perish," doesn't suggest physical death, but people without vision are living unintentionally and are preparing themselves to live with regret.

Do not limit yourself. Dream big. There is always a pathway to your vision. The bigger the vision, the bigger the peril, but those who dream big and overcome the most challenging perils reap the greatest rewards. *(See Appendix, Item F for questions that will serve as a guide for you to develop your own personal vision.)*

Once you've written your answers to the questions in Appendix, Item F, you must evaluate them and ask yourself one additional question: How will I know if I've fulfilled my vision? You must be able to measure whether or not you are fulfilling your vision. If you can't, you will not be able to direct your disciplines appropriately. I recommend that you ask a mentor, coach, or peer to help you. That will help you improve clarity and set yourself in a good direction.

Once you have settled on a way to measure your progress, choose one area to focus on, whichever draws your attention the most, and then map out an action plan. We use the SMART goal methodology:

- **S**pecific: Clearly define what you want to achieve.
- **M**easurable: Establish criteria to track progress and success.
- **A**chievable: Set realistic and attainable goals.
- **R**elevant: Ensure goals align with your overall objectives and aspirations.
- **T**ime-bound: Assign a specific timeframe for goal completion, creating focus and urgency.

Download our complimentary SMART goal-mapping tool from www.theleadershipedgebook.com. Take a few of your goals and go through the exercise. When you have finished, you are ready to take action through systematic disciplines.

- *Disciplines:* Two of my favorite quotes on discipline are from Jim Rohm, an American entrepreneur, author, and motivational speaker: "Discipline weighs ounces, but regret weighs a ton," and "Success is a few simple disciplines repeated every day."

The difference between discipline and regret is small daily choices that when compounded over time create a large gap between success and failure. For example:

- Business:
  - Discipline: Consistently setting and reviewing goals, maintaining a structured work schedule, and implementing effective time management strategies.
  - Regret: Failing to invest in continuous learning and skill development, missing out on opportunities due to fear of failure or indecisiveness, and neglecting to build a strong professional network.

- Health:
  - Discipline: Regular exercise routine, balanced and nutritious diet, consistent sleep patterns, and proactive health check-ups.
  - Regret: Ignoring warning signs of health issues, neglecting self-care and stress management, indulging in unhealthy habits, and failing to prioritize mental well-being.
- Relationships:
  - Discipline: Active listening, effective communication, regular quality time with loved ones, practicing empathy and understanding.
  - Regret: Taking relationships for granted, not expressing appreciation or affection, failing to resolve conflicts constructively, and prioritizing work or personal interests over nurturing relationships.

A life of discipline or regret is built on basic choices: to be kind or rude; to confront or retreat; to connect or isolate; to take risks or play it safe. The most influential leaders are those who make powerful choices. They choose to serve rather than be served, to live for purpose before profits, to persevere instead of give up, and to forgive instead of becoming resentful.

Your Value System for Decision Making

Every decision we make has a value system behind it. C.S. Lewis said, "Education without values, as useful as it is, seems rather to make a man a more clever devil." Before you take action toward fulfilling your purpose and vision, you must determine your values. Values are like guard rails on the motorway; they keep you from veering off the road and over the edge. They determine how far you'll go on questionable issues. Knowing and living your values is the key to being a leader worth following and living a life of purpose. Most people know their values; the challenge is intentionally and habitually using them as filters and guides in decision making. Everyone values honesty, integrity, and respect, but the question is, do we really live those values, especially when doing so makes demands on us?

I suggest that you build your value system on what you can control: your attitude, effort, and cooperation. Attitude is a settled way of thinking or feeling about someone or something, typically one that is reflected in a person's behavior. Effort is a rigorous or determined attempt. Cooperation is working together toward the same end.

Attitude, effort, and cooperation work symbiotically. Attitude directs effort and cooperation, then effort and cooperation influence attitude. In short, what we think is what we feel is what we do. According to dozens of success experts, a positive attitude is the main factor in becoming a successful leader.

From 2013 to 2018, I was coaching and consulting for a franchise network. I was contracted by the corporate office to reach out to each franchise owner once each month to see if I could help them spark growth in their franchise.

Shawn and Ted, both from the Dallas/Fort Worth metropolitan area, had owned their respective franchises for more than five years and were generating just under a million dollars annually in revenue. They were both riddled with negative attitudes. They blamed their lack of success on the area, the corporate office, the products, and the lack of good workers. Their attitude affected their effort, and instead of trying new methods or ways to do things, they made excuses and kept repeating unsuccessful behaviors. It also affected their cooperation, as they were hostile toward the corporate office, which was trying to help them, and toward their own staff.

However, from 2014 to 2016, Shawn and Ted went in two different directions. Shawn grew his franchise to $2.7 million in revenue and increased his profits from around 15 to 22 percent. Ted went in the opposite direction. He went from just under a million dollars in sales to around a half million, to under a half a million, to selling his franchise to Shawn. He perpetually talked about his lack of opportunity, lack of resources, and lack of "good people."

The only difference between the two was attitude. Shawn entered 2014 determined to change his attitude. Up to that point, he did not believe he could reach over a million dollars per year. I had spent hours talking to him in 2013 about how he could not only surpass a million but whatever number he determined. While I showed him logical, simple, practical, and systematic ways to grow his sales, he was struggling to let go of negativity. But at the beginning of 2014, he changed his attitude and followed through with action. Within two years, he tripled his revenue, increased his profit, and built systems of duplication for his staff that led to more fulfilled, engaged, and entrepreneurial mindsets among his team.

Turning Thoughts Into Actions

Logic is the language of our mind. Emotion is the language of our body. Action is a reaction to what we think and feel. We filter each thought through our brain's reticular activating system, which increases our focus on that thought, which is then channeled through our limbic system, and a combination of chemicals is released, which causes us to feel a variety of ways.

When we feel something, we are compelled to act. The chemicals we allow to be filtered into our body then determine the actions we take, which creates results. As we think the same thoughts, feel the same emotions, and do the same things over and over again, habits of thinking, feeling, and acting are forged. Once habits are forged, we react subconsciously. When we get undesired results, we feel powerless, and the tendency is to blame outside circumstances, complain about the lack of opportunity, deflect responsibility, and make excuses for why we are getting undesired results. BCDE are the results of powerless habitual thoughts, emotions, and actions.

But habits can be changed. Human beings never lose plasticity or the ability to elevate their thoughts, emotions, or actions, regardless of their circumstances. No matter how you think, feel, or are compelled to act, you never *have* to act.

Having a positive attitude is simply changing your perspective of your circumstances. You often don't have a choice in your circumstances, and you don't have to like your circumstances, but you do choose your attitude in every circumstance, which will determine the way you feel about your circumstances, which will help you make good choices.

To be an effective self-leader, you must choose in every circumstance to focus on what you want versus what you don't want. This can be challenging, especially when those around you are consumed by negativity.

Your attitude is your choice; that choice will ultimately determine your success or failure.

Take these steps to help you build your personal value system for a positive attitude:

- Reflect: Take some time to reflect on your current attitudes and how they impact your life. Consider situations when you felt positive and when negativity took over. Identify areas where you want to improve your attitude.
- Identify positive attitudes: List the attitudes and behaviors that you associate with positivity. These could include optimism, gratitude, kindness, resilience, open-mindedness, and a willingness to learn from challenges.
- Clarify your core values: Determine your core values that align with a positive attitude. For example, you might value self-improvement, empathy, compassion, or a sense of humor.
- Set positive intentions: Define your intentions for maintaining a positive attitude in specific situations. Intentions act as guiding principles for your behavior and reactions.
- Practice self-awareness: Pay attention to your thoughts and emotions regularly. Notice when negative thoughts arise and practice redirecting them toward more positive and constructive perspectives. (*The Leadership Edge* will address this in greater detail in Chapter 7.)
- Foster a growth mindset: Embrace the idea that challenges are opportunities for growth and learning. Value effort and perseverance in the face of setbacks.
- Surround yourself with positive influences: Engage with people who have a positive attitude and can support and inspire you on your journey.
- Regularly review and adjust: Revisit your personal value system weekly. I recommend writing your value system out and evaluating yourself on a sliding scale each week to keep track of how you're doing. I highly recommend doing this

with a mentor, coach, or peer. As you grow and change, your values and attitudes may evolve too.

What does a positive attitude value system look like? How does it exhibit itself? A few thoughts on how to maintain a positive attitude:

- Optimism: There are positive aspects to most situations; I focus on finding solutions rather than dwelling on problems.
- Gratitude: I express gratitude for the blessings in my life and actively seek opportunities to appreciate the little things.
- Resilience: I view challenges as opportunities to learn and grow, and I embrace setbacks as part of the journey to success.
- Compassion: I show understanding and empathy toward others, recognizing that everyone has their struggles.
- Adaptability: I'm open-minded and willing to adapt to new circumstances, embracing change as a chance for growth.
- Self-improvement: I value continuous self-improvement and see failures as stepping stones toward personal development.

What does a negative value system look like? Nobody writes these down. These happen subconsciously, as we've discussed, but recognizing them will help you catch yourself if you're violating your values.

- Pessimism: I often expect the worst outcome in most situations and find it hard to see the positive side.
- Complaining: I tend to focus on what's wrong rather than appreciating what's right, leading to constant complaints.
- Helplessness: I feel defeated by challenges and believe that my efforts won't make a difference.
- Judgmental: I often criticize others without understanding their perspectives, leading to strained relationships.
- Resistance to change: I resist change and prefer to stay in my comfort zone, even if it hinders my personal growth.
- Self-doubt: I doubt my abilities and tend to give up easily when faced with obstacles.

Now, write down what you value, and be intentional about writing statements that will remind you of how you want to act in challenging circumstances. Cultivating a value system is an ongoing process that requires effort, self-awareness, and ongoing evaluation. By building a value system that prioritizes positivity, you can elevate the thoughts, emotions, and actions that will guide you through the challenges of fulfilling your purpose and vision.

Chapter 6 Takeaways

- Self-leadership is the most important, challenging, and rewarding leadership discipline of all.
- Everyone in a free-market system is a business owner, and everyone is responsible for the choices they make, and the value they bring to the marketplace, increasing their value, having a positive attitude, giving their best effort, and fostering cooperation.
- Effective leaders focus on what they can control, and in life, there are only three things you can control: your own attitude, your own effort, and your own level of cooperation.
- The bigger the vision, the bigger the peril, but those who dream big and overcome the most challenging perils reap the greatest rewards.
- The most influential leaders are those who make powerful choices: to serve rather than be served, to live for purpose before profits, to persevere instead of give up, and to forgive instead of becoming resentful.

CHAPTER 7

Know Yourself to Lead Yourself

Socrates emphasized the importance of self-knowledge and self-reflection in his teachings through directives like "Know thyself" and "The unexamined life is not worth living." These proverb-like statements encapsulate the importance of self-knowledge and the significance of introspection. When he advised his followers to "Know thyself," he was advising them to engage in self-examination for a better understanding of their true natures.

Self-knowledge involves exploring one's natural propensities, values, beliefs, strengths, weaknesses, desires, and limitations. By truly understanding ourselves, we can make better choices, live in accordance with our values, and lead more meaningful lives. Self-knowledge is a key discipline for leadership growth and fulfillment.

Socrates' statement that "The unexamined life is not worth living" reflects the belief that a life devoid of self-reflection and critical examination lacks true purpose and value. People who do not question their beliefs, actions, and assumptions live a superficial and unfulfilling existence. Self-reflection and examination enable us to uncover ignorance, challenge our preconceived notions, and seek wisdom. An examined life involves constant inquiry, the pursuit of truth, and the willingness to confront and question oneself.

Self-knowledge and self-examination advocate for a life of intellectual and moral integrity. Leaders who actively engage in self-reflection and seek knowledge about themselves are better equipped to make better decisions, live in the present, and contribute positively to their organizations.

Self-Knowledge Disciplines

Self-Knowledge Discipline #1: Personality assessments

Personality assessments are tools to help people understand their natural propensities, strengths, weaknesses, opportunities, and threats. Understanding your personality will allow you to become more aware of your personal "best practices" for navigating the circumstances you will face as a leader. There is no one-size-fits-all leadership approach; it is one-size-fits-one.

At the foundational level, personality tests measure two things:

1. Introversion and extroversion.
2. Task orientation and people orientation.

Everyone is a combination of the two, but you want to understand what your natural propensity is. For example, if you are reserved in social settings but genuinely care about people and tend to connect with people on a deeper level, your primary combination is introverted and people-oriented. This doesn't mean you cannot be extroverted or task-oriented; it just means your default position is to be introverted and people-oriented. This is vital to know, understand, and accept in order to lead yourself better in relationships, at work, and in achievements. Far too many people spend far too much time comparing themselves to others instead of getting to know and leading themselves toward their best.

Let's consider each personality type and combination.

Extroversion

An extrovert is energized by social interactions and thrives in dynamic, outgoing environments. For instance, at a party, they eagerly engage in conversations, exuding enthusiasm and confidence. They enjoy meeting new people, making friends effortlessly, and are often the life of the gathering. In group settings, they actively participate, sharing ideas and seeking others' opinions. An extrovert can be the one to initiate group activities or games, encouraging everyone to join in the fun. They are expressive and comfortable with public speaking, often taking the lead in presentations or discussions. Their outgoing nature fosters connections, making them approachable and well-liked by many different kinds of people.

Introversion

An introvert finds solace in solitary activities and tends to recharge through "alone time." After a long day at work, they might retreat to a quiet space to read a book or engage in a creative hobby. In social gatherings, they can initially appear reserved, taking time to observe and get comfortable with the surroundings and people. While they value close and meaningful relationships, they often prefer one-on-one conversations over large group interactions. Introverts excel in introspection and critical thinking, appreciating the chance to process their thoughts internally. Their ability to focus and listen attentively makes them excellent listeners and thoughtful problem-solvers.

Task Orientation

A task-oriented person approaches activities with a structured and goal-driven mindset. For example, when planning a vacation, they first define their objective: relaxation, adventure, and cultural exploration. Next, they meticulously research destinations, considering factors like travel time, budget, and available activities. Once they have gathered their options, they prioritize them based on preferences and goal alignment. Creating a detailed itinerary, they organize daily activities, accommodations, and transportation arrangements. During the trip, they manage time effectively and quickly find solutions to obstacles. Afterwards, they reflect on the experience, evaluating whether they achieved their initial goal and learning from the process for future endeavors.

People Orientation

A people-oriented person is highly attuned to the needs and emotions of others. For instance, in a team project, they prioritize building strong interpersonal relationships among team members. They actively listen to their colleagues' ideas and concerns, fostering an inclusive and collaborative environment. Such individuals excel at resolving conflicts and promoting harmony within the group. They empathize with their teammates, understand their strengths and weaknesses, and assign tasks accordingly to bring out the best in each member. Additionally, they celebrate others' successes genuinely and offer support during challenging times. Their focus on building positive connections creates a cohesive and motivated team, contributing to overall success and a nurturing work environment.

Extroversion With a Task Orientation

An extrovert who is task-oriented exhibits a unique blend of outgoing energy and goal-oriented focus. For instance, when assigned a team project, they actively engage with their colleagues, fostering a positive and collaborative atmosphere. They enjoy brainstorming sessions and animated discussions, using their social skills to bring out the best ideas from the group. However, despite their sociable nature, they keep the team firmly on track toward achieving objectives. They skillfully delegate tasks, considering each member's strengths, and ensure effective communication throughout the project. Their ability to motivate others and maintain a sense of camaraderie helps the team stay driven and achieve successful outcomes. Some positions that suit their personality traits:

- Human resources manager: They can effectively handle employee relations, training, and organizational development.
- Marketing manager: Their ability to strategize and connect with others aids in creating and implementing successful marketing campaigns.
- Customer service manager: They enjoy resolving customer issues, leading a team, and maintaining high levels of customer satisfaction.
- Business development manager: They thrive in identifying growth opportunities and nurturing partnerships with clients and stakeholders.

Introversion With a Task Orientation

An introvert who is task-oriented displays a quiet determination and a focused approach to achieving goals. For example, when given a challenging project, they prefer to work independently, valuing the solitude that allows them to concentrate deeply on the task at hand. They meticulously plan and organize their work, breaking it down into manageable steps. Their excellent time management skills ensure they stay on schedule and meet deadlines effectively. While they may not seek the spotlight, their work speaks for itself, showcasing their dedication and attention to detail. Their introspective nature allows them to find innovative solutions and excel in problem-solving, making them reliable and efficient contributors to any team. Some careers that suit their personality traits:

- Data analyst: They thrive in roles that involve analyzing and interpreting data to provide valuable insights and recommendations.
- Accountant: Their meticulous nature makes them well-suited for managing financial records and ensuring accuracy in financial reporting.
- Quality assurance specialist: They are adept at ensuring products and services meet high standards through rigorous testing and analysis.
- Graphic designer/artist: Their creativity and task-oriented approach make them skilled in producing visually appealing and well-planned designs.

Extroversion With a People Orientation

An extrovert who is people-oriented thrives on building meaningful connections and fostering a supportive environment for others. For instance, in a team setting, they are the approachable and empathetic colleague, always ready to lend a listening ear and offer assistance. They excel at networking and effortlessly expand their social circle, making everyone feel valued and included. In group discussions, they actively engage with team members, encouraging diverse perspectives and collaboration. Their enthusiastic nature lifts team morale, and they celebrate others' achievements genuinely. This extroverted individual is attuned to the emotional needs of their peers, skillfully mediating conflicts and promoting a harmonious atmosphere, which ultimately contributes to a cohesive and motivated team. Some jobs that suit their personality traits:

- Sales representative: Their outgoing nature and ability to connect with others make them excellent at building rapport with potential clients and closing deals.
- Public relations manager: Their strong interpersonal skills enable them to effectively manage relationships with the media, clients, and the public.
- Training and development specialist: Their extroverted nature makes them great at delivering engaging training sessions and workshops for employees.
- Recruiter: They enjoy networking and connecting with potential candidates, matching them with suitable job opportunities.

Introversion With a People Orientation

In a work setting, the introverted, people-oriented individual may initially appear reserved, but they excel at building strong and productive relationships with their colleagues. They actively listen during meetings and discussions, considering others' viewpoints before expressing their own valuable insights. While they may not seek the spotlight, they willingly collaborate with teammates, recognizing the importance of collective success. This introverted team member is a trusted and empathetic listener, offering support and encouragement to their peers during challenging times. They contribute to a harmonious work environment by mediating conflicts with tact and understanding. Despite their preference for solitude, their people-oriented nature shines through in their genuine care for the well-being and growth of their co-workers. Some jobs that would suit their personality traits:

- Counselor or therapist: Their empathetic and attentive nature makes them well-suited for providing support and guidance to individuals seeking help.
- Social worker: They thrive in roles that involve advocating for and assisting vulnerable or disadvantaged populations.
- Personal trainer: Their ability to connect with clients on a personal level helps them provide tailored fitness guidance and support.
- Veterinarian or animal caretaker: Their love for animals allows them to provide compassionate care to pets and build a strong bond with them.

There are dozens of personality tests that psychologists, sociologists, and behavioral scientists have created for people to get to know themselves. My recommendation is to take as many as possible and study them vigilantly. My team uses the DISC (dominance, influence, steadiness, conscientiousness) personality profile for deep dives with clients and for workshops and seminars. But to get started quickly, take the five-minute Smalley and Trent Personality test. It is very similar to DISC in structure, and it is simple, printable, easily accessible, and available at everyone's favorite price: free. You can access it through any search engine. Download the PDF, take the test, and then review your results immediately. The Smalley and Trent test is a quick way to increase your self-knowledge.

Of course, everyone exhibits something of each personality type, but the goal is to discover where your natural propensities are and where you give and receive the most energy. Once you make that discovery, it's important to recognize, acknowledge, and accept it. I have many clients who read their personality assessment and then shame themselves because they have thought they needed to be something different. Don't be a self-shamer; celebrate who you are! You have never needed to be anyone but yourself. Self-awareness unlocks potential. When you accept who you are, you can begin to channel it through your personal and organizational PVD and work in line with your strengths as often as possible.

Be an avid student of yourself. Don't stop with DISC or a five-minute test. Whenever you have an opportunity to take a personality test, I recommend you do so. And as a leader doing the work of self-discovery, I encourage you to invite your team to take the journey with you.

Self-Knowledge Discipline #2: Journaling

Author Christina Baldwin writes, "Journaling is the voyage to the interior." Journaling allows people to see themselves from a third-party perspective as they delve into their thoughts, emotions, and experiences, fostering a deeper understanding of themselves. Journaling is a practice we initiate with all our clients.

My colleagues and I have countless stories of how journaling increases self-awareness and improves self-leadership. One of those stories is about Sara, a talented and capable middle-level manager who wanted greater leadership responsibilities but was not being promoted. Sara was frustrated and asked her leaders for feedback as to why she was being passed up for promotions. Her leaders told her that her communication style was harsh and critical, and team members did not respond well to her.

At first, Sara was frustrated by the feedback and excused her style as "just being honest." One of our consultants advised her to journal about her leaders, colleagues, and herself and then to read her journal entries out loud. Sara followed the advice, and as she did, she noticed how harsh, critical, and judgmental her language was as she wrote about others. But to Sara's surprise, the words in her journal about herself were particularly critical.

With that self-awareness, she went to work on being intentionally gracious toward others and herself. Her communication style softened, her leaders noticed the change, and she was later offered a promotion.

Journaling not only improves self-awareness but also serves as a therapeutic outlet for releasing stress and anxiety, providing emotional release and promoting mental clarity. It contributes to memory enhancement, facilitating the retention and recall of significant events. As Lord Bacon wrote, "Reading makes a learned man, but writing makes a precise man."

Additionally, journaling supports personal growth, goal setting, and decision making while promoting stress management, improved communication, and the identification of patterns and habits.

If you aren't currently journaling, here is a simple process for getting started:

- Purchase a journal. I suggest a leather-bound journal with a penholder and a high-quality pen. Having a high-quality pen will help you be more cognizant of the instrument and its purpose.
- Commit to writing in your journal every day; perhaps in the morning before you start your day, or as a reflection exercise before you go to sleep.
- Begin writing by answering questions, such as:
  - What's going on of significance to your life?
  - What are you excited about today?
  - What is worrying you?
  - What are you grateful for today?
  - Who are you grateful to today?
  - What's one change you want to see in the world today?
  - What are you going to do today to help move the needle on that change?
- Read your entries out loud for a "third party" view into your heart and mind. It will help you identify times when you're giving into blaming, complaining, deflection, and excuses.
- Reframe negativity. When you identify negative thoughts, question their accuracy and validity. Ask yourself if there is evidence to support or refute them. Often, negativity is a distorted view, based on assumptions rather than reality. Once you catch those thoughts, redirect them. I personally use the "probable versus possible method."

When I'm swirling in negativity, it is usually because I have made a mistake, like forgetting to respond to a client's question or missing a detail in a report. I usually begin expecting the worst possible outcome, such as the client firing me, badmouthing me, and going on a rampage to destroy me. When I catch myself doing this, I stop, take a deep breath and ask, "Is it possible your client would react like this?" Then I follow up with the question, "Is it probable?" This snaps me out of my negative swirl and allows me to think logically about how I can own my mistake and deliver what I promised.

Self-Knowledge Discipline #3: Peer feedback

Peer feedback is vital to getting to know yourself well; it helps us expose our self-knowledge blind spots. The concept of blind spots was originally presented through the Johari Window, a model created in 1955 by psychologists Joseph Luft and Harry Ingham. It provides a framework for understanding and improving interpersonal communication and self-awareness.

The Johari Window divides an individual's self-awareness into four "quadrants" or panes, representing different aspects of knowledge and information about oneself:

1. Open or Arena: Represents the information that is known to both the individual and others. It includes the individual's attitudes, behaviors, feelings, and other personal characteristics that are readily visible and openly communicated.
2. Hidden or Façade: Contains information about the individual that is known to the person but not to others. It represents things like secrets, private thoughts, and personal experiences that the individual chooses not to share openly.
3. Blind Spot: Contains information about the individual realized by others but not by them. It represents aspects of their behavior, attitude, or impact on others that they are unaware of. Feedback from others can help individuals expand their self-awareness in this area.
4. Unknown: Represents information that is unknown to both the individual and others. It includes unconscious motives, repressed memories, or aspects of personality that have not yet been discovered or explored.

The goal of the Johari Window is to increase the size of the open quadrant by sharing information about oneself with others, receiving feedback, and expanding self-awareness. By doing so, individuals can reduce their blind spots, uncover hidden aspects of themselves, and improve their communications and relationships.

Discussing your thoughts, emotions, and ideas and getting feedback from a trusted person who knows you and cares about you is one of the best ways to reveal blind spots and expand self-awareness. We spend our entire lives in our own minds, emotions, and bodies. It is difficult to know how others view us unless we ask them and are open to their feedback—both positive and negative.

Here's a step-by-step guide on how to create a constructive and supportive environment that welcomes honest feedback:

- Set clear objectives: Clearly communicate the purpose of seeking feedback: knowing yourself better and improving your personal growth. Encourage participants to be candid, emphasizing that their feedback should be constructive and focused on personal development.
- Choose the right feedback providers: Select peers and mentors you trust and respect. Ensure they have a good understanding of your strengths, weaknesses, and work dynamics. You can share your personality assessments and your PVD to help those who are giving you feedback understand you better. Diverse perspectives from different people can provide a well-rounded view.
- Use specific questions: Provide focused questions that prompt targeted feedback, such as:
  o What do you think are my top strengths and the areas where I need improvement?
  o What do you think of my communication style and collaboration skills?
  o What actions or behaviors do you think I could change to be more effective in my role?

- Anonymous or confidential feedback: Offer participants the option to provide anonymous or confidential feedback if they feel more comfortable sharing their insights without attribution. This can lead to more honest responses and can work particularly well with a group of people you are leading.
- Timing and frequency: Choose an appropriate time to seek feedback, ideally after a significant project or milestone. Additionally, consider periodic feedback sessions to track your progress over time.
- Active listening: Receive feedback with an open mind and actively listen to the insights shared. Avoid getting defensive; instead, ask clarifying questions to fully understand the feedback.
- Reflect: Take time to reflect on the feedback you receive. Look for patterns and common themes in the responses to gain a deeper understanding of yourself.
- Acknowledge and appreciate: Express gratitude to those who provided feedback. Let them know you value their input and that it will help you grow as a person and professional.
- Create an action plan: Based on the feedback, create an action plan to work on areas of improvement and leverage your strengths. Set specific, achievable goals and establish a timeline for progress.
- follow-up: Keep your peers and mentors informed about your progress. Share how their feedback has influenced your development. This encourages a sense of their involvement and accountability in your growth journey.

When you first start this process, it is easy to become defensive and make excuses. Nobody likes negative feedback. But great leaders lean into the pain to create better solutions for themselves and others.

Self-Examination Disciplines

Benjamin Franklin practiced self-examination through a technique he called "The Art of Virtue." He created a list of 13 virtues he aimed to cultivate in himself, including temperance, silence, order, and sincerity.

Each week, he focused on one virtue, carefully observing his behavior and progress. Franklin kept a journal to record his daily successes and failures, reflecting on his actions and striving for self-improvement. This practice of self-reflection and continuous self-improvement was an essential part of his personal development and contributed to his success as a statesman, inventor, and philosopher.

Self-knowledge is essential if you are going to be an effective leader; self-examination is just as important. As you become more intentional in fulfilling your PVD and living your value system, you are going to face challenges that open you to the option of discipline or compromise. And you will compromise your values at times. To keep yourself on track, intentional, and disciplined, you must take time to examine your progress and rate yourself—and take mental "do-overs."

In creating your self-examination "system," the goal is to make self-examination a habitual and fluid part of your life. The more you practice self-examination, the easier it will be for you to identify your thoughts, emotions, and actions. Here are some steps you can take:

- Like Benjamin Franklin, develop a rating system checklist of your values, purpose, and vision. Before you rate yourself, you will want to disconnect from technology, be "present," and reflect on the day, week, or month. How people become present varies. Some of our clients practice deep breathing and meditation. Others go for a walk. Some go to a quiet room and sit in the same chair each examination session. And others work out and examine themselves after they've cooled off. There is no one method for everyone. Try them all, find one that suits you, and stick to it.

Once you're present and reflecting, rate yourself on a sliding scale of 1 to 5 (1 = lowest, 5 = highest) on how intentional you have been during the period of time you are examining in living your values, purpose, and making progress toward your vision. Then, if you find that you've compromised your values in any way, close your eyes and allow yourself to go back to the moment of compromise and conduct a "do-over." A do-over is an exercise of mental and emotional rehearsal.

It will prime your mind and body to react differently if you are in that situation again.

Consider this example of a mental and emotional do-over for someone who compromised their values at work:

- The compromise: Jane, a dedicated and ethical employee, is put in a challenging situation. Her boss instructs her to manipulate financial data to make the company's financial performance appear better than it is. Jane feels pressured and fears losing her job if she refuses to comply, so she compromises her values by doing what her boss instructs. Jane immediately regrets her decision and is filled with guilt and shame.
- Later, she conducts a mental and emotional do-over to rehearse how she will respond the next time she is requested to manipulate company financial data.
  - The mental do-over: Instead of succumbing to the pressure, Jane decides to take a step back and reflect on her values and the potential consequences of compromising them. She reminds herself of the importance of honesty, integrity, and the long-term impact of her actions. With a clear mindset, she focuses on finding alternative solutions that align with her principles while addressing her boss's concerns.
  - The emotional do-over: Recognizing the stress and emotional turmoil caused by this dilemma, Jane takes time to manage her emotions constructively. She talks to a trusted colleague or friend to share her concerns and gain support. She practices self-compassion, acknowledging the difficulty of the situation while maintaining self-respect and self-worth. Then Jane tells her boss she understands he is under a lot of pressure, but she doesn't feel comfortable compromising her values and manipulating financial data. In her rehearsal, she accepts any consequence that might come with her decision. As she does this, she feels peace in knowing that she won't make such a compromise again.
- Together, mental and emotional do-overs enable Jane to stay true to her values and find a way to handle the situation with

integrity. By approaching the challenge from a place of clarity and emotional resilience, Jane can navigate future workplace dilemmas while maintaining her ethical standards and preserving her peace of mind.

Do-overs are an extremely powerful examination exercise because we train our bodies and minds to react in alignment with our values. We are essentially deciding ahead of time what we will do in various circumstances and teaching ourselves to lean into the pain of discipline to avoid the pain of regret.

- Next, examine how intentional you were in living your purpose. Reflect on the key areas where you intentionally thought about, acted on, and communicated in alignment with your purpose. The more you examine this introspectively, the more you will consider your purpose when making decisions. If you make decisions out of alignment with your purpose, reflect on it, write it out in your journal, and recommit to living from your purpose.
- Finally, track any and all progress you've made toward your vision. Be specific. Review your SMART Goal Map and check off any items you have accomplished. For example, if a part of your vision is to help each of your team members set and achieve their personal goals, and you have met with a team member to discuss and review their goals, that was taking a step toward your vision. Write it down, and mark it as progress. Then reflect on what you did, and consider how you might improve on what you did and how you might take those improvements to more team members. If you made no progress, consider how you can discipline yourself to make progress and make plans to do so.

Values	Scale 1-5	Do-overs?
Purpose	Scale 1-5	Intentionality?
Vision	Scale 1-5	Progress?

Figure 7.1 Values, Purpose, Values Scale

To download the high-performance self-examination tool, please visit www.theleadershipedgebook.com.

- Frequency: The goal is for self-examination to be a fluid part of your life. Eventually, you want to reflect in real time, where you can identify emotions before making poor decisions, conduct rehearsals prior to responding to challenges, and catch compromises in the moment and amend them. Until then, consider these recommendations for building the habit of self-examination:
  - Daily: Spend 15 minutes at the end of every day examining your day using the steps above.
  - Weekly: Spend one hour at the end of every week in broader reflection. Reflect on patterns of thoughts, behaviors, and communication that are in alignment with your PVD and value system, then reflect on patterns that led you away from them.
  - Monthly: Spend three hours at the end of every month reflecting on a broader scale. I suggest you do a portion of this with a peer, coach, or mentor. Use this time to review your SMART Goal Map in more detail and put specific action items in your calendar or planner for the following month.

A final note on self-knowledge and self-examination: As you practice the disciplines outlined in this chapter, you will begin to change the way you think, behave, and communicate. You will see better results in your work and become sharper in your examination of those you work with. You will be more fulfilled and excited and want to share those newfound feelings with your peers, but I caution you not to force these practices on those around you. These disciplines can expose unresolved traumas; people can easily become defensive. Allow them to observe your progress and reflect on their own. Remember that leadership is influence; the more you grow in self-discipline, the more your results will influence others to want to follow you.

Chapter 7 Takeaways

- Self-knowledge is a key discipline for leadership growth and fulfillment.
- An examined life involves constant inquiry, the pursuit of truth, and the willingness to confront and question oneself.
- Personality assessments are tools to help people understand their natural propensities, strengths, weaknesses, opportunities, and threats.
- Journaling allows people to see themselves from a third-party perspective as they delve into their thoughts, emotions, and experiences, fostering a deeper understanding of themselves.
- Peer feedback is vital to getting to know yourself well; it helps us expose our self-knowledge blind spots.
- Self-knowledge is essential if you are going to be an effective leader; self-examination is just as important.
- Do-overs are an extremely powerful examination exercise because we train our bodies and minds to react in alignment with our values.
- Leadership is influence; the more you grow in self-discipline, the more your results will influence others to want to follow you.

CHAPTER 8

LEAD Your Days

We've all heard the saying, "Live each day as if it were your last." But in the midst of life's complexities, chaos, and monotony, each day can feel like it's no different from the last and has no relevance to tomorrow. The more we allow outside forces to dictate our direction and quality of life, the easier it is to accept that a day is just a day and not a precious construct of minutes and hours to be used for our own benefit and that of others.

I'm writing this chapter after just having lost my Dad to a heart attack. I would like nothing more than to be able to spend one more day with him. If we had one more day together, I would tell him how grateful I am for his fierce love, the lessons he taught me, his unrelenting pursuit of purpose, and his undying devotion to self-leadership. I would sit and talk with him about our favorite football teams. I would talk to him about leadership and other topics he was passionate about. I would not take a moment for granted.

We've all lost someone we wish we could have had one more day with. It's easy to make grandiose proclamations at funerals or wakes about how our loss has changed us and that we're no longer going to take time, relationships, or opportunities for granted. But it's even easier, and more likely, that after a few days or weeks, we will return to our old habit of taking things for granted. Not to discount the sincerity of our proclamations, but unless we change our daily patterns, unless we create new thoughts, behaviors, and communication, nothing will change.

Each day is precious and deserves intention. You've heard people say, "I'm just trying to get through the day." Even more often, I engage with people who are counting the hours, minutes, and seconds until they can leave work for a few hours of reprieve before they go to sleep to get up and do the same thing the next day. It's a sad squandering of the precious time they have to "give to the day" as opposed to "get through the day."

Everything discussed here in Part 2 on self-leadership is designed to help you LEAD Your Days, to be intentional and practical in applying the various concepts addressed here. Unless we are committed to this process, to applying what we know about self-leadership each day, we will never become the type of leaders people want to follow. Leadership without discipline is dangerous. Discipline sustains leadership.

The LEAD Your Days process is a work in progress. As discussed elsewhere in *The Leadership Edge*, you need to make this tool uniquely yours. Find out what works for you and what doesn't; continue to refine your process. If it works for you as I define it here, fine, but you have the ultimate say in how you LEAD Your Days. One thing is unequivocal: to be an effective leader, you must be intentional about how you LEAD Your Days.

The LEAD System

Hall of Fame football coach Don Shula used to say, "It's the start that stops most people." According to a study by the Tracy Group,[1] those who consistently plan their days are 50 percent more productive than those who don't, but unfortunately, according to numerous studies, fewer than 20 percent of people plan their days. If you want to be productive, you must plan, prioritize, and examine. We recommend a program we call LEAD, an acrostic that stands for:

L—Listen
E—Engage gratitude
A—Adopt one person per day to encourage
D—Determine priorities (with the PVD planning tool)

L—Listen: When you wake up, spend the first 30 minutes of your day listening. Listen to your thoughts and feelings; listen to the sounds of nature or sounds around your house; or embrace silence. Allow yourself to *listen* to your insight. This means no cell phone calls for those 30 minutes. Don't be one of the 89 percent of people who check their phones within 10 minutes of waking up, who commit their brains to murky waters first thing in the morning.

The brain generates electrical activity. These electrical patterns are known as brainwaves and are measured using an electroencephalogram (EEG). There are five main types of brainwave patterns, each associated with different mental states and activities. As a part of self-awareness and self-regulation, it's important to understand them so you can understand why it's so important to keep the first 30 minutes of your day free of contrast:

- Beta waves are associated with active, alert, and focused states of consciousness. They are most dominant when we are awake, engaged in cognitive tasks, problem-solving, or interacting with the external environment. High-frequency beta waves are linked to heightened concentration and mental alertness.
- Alpha waves occur when we are in a relaxed and calm state but still awake and conscious. They are often associated with a meditative state, daydreaming, or a state of effortless attention. Alpha waves can be beneficial for promoting creativity, stress reduction, and a sense of relaxation.
- Theta waves are generated during light sleep, deep meditation, and states of deep relaxation. They are associated with the early stages of sleep and are also present during deep, creative visualization or during moments of insight and inspiration. Theta waves are thought to be connected to accessing the subconscious mind.
- Delta waves are the slowest brainwave pattern and are associated with deep, dreamless sleep and unconsciousness. They are crucial for restorative sleep and physical healing. Delta waves help the body and mind rejuvenate and replenish energy.
- Gamma waves are the fastest brainwave pattern and are associated with high-level cognitive processing and integration of information from various brain regions. They are linked to advanced mental activities, heightened perception, and moments of insight and inspiration. Gamma waves are also believed to play a role in enhancing memory and learning.

Your goal is to spend the majority of your days in alpha brainwaves, where you are calm, mindful, creative, clear, and conscious. In alpha brainwave states, you are more productive and thoughtful, and you work faster. However, we live in a society that promotes high beta brainwaves as a means for higher production. Being "busy" is a badge of honor, and if you're not busy, you can be judged as nonproductive or even lazy. According to neuroscientist Dr. Joe Dispenza,[2] people spend more than 80 percent of their days in mid-high beta brainwave states. An increase in beta waves increases stress levels in two ways:

1. An overactive mind: High-frequency beta waves are associated with an overactive mind, which can lead to excessive thinking, worry, and rumination. Such mental chatter can contribute to feelings of anxiety and stress.
2. Chronic stress: Prolonged exposure to stressful situations can lead to increased beta-wave activity, especially in the prefrontal cortex. This heightened beta activity is linked to chronic stress, which can have detrimental effects on physical and mental well-being.

When you wake up, you go from delta to theta brainwaves where you're relaxed, creative, and meditative. When you look at your cell phone first thing in the morning, you bypass theta and move right into a beta state, which awakens you to the five senses and catapults your mind and body into action. Often, this leads to cluttered thoughts, feeling overwhelmed, and hastiness. The goal every morning is to be clear-minded and allow thoughts to come and go as they please. Listening to yourself is a great gift, not only to yourself but to those you lead. Our world is unfathomably cluttered with overstimulation. Listening allows you the chance to engage your critical thinking skills, which is your leadership problem-solving funnel. Protect the first 30 minutes of your day as if the quality of your day depends on it because it does.

E—Engage Gratitude

Gratitude is our body's natural combatant against fear, doubt, and worry. Housed in our brain's limbic system is a synapse (the brain's connection points) called the amygdala. The amygdala integrates our body with emotions, emotional behavior, and motivation. Emotional behavior is largely affected by the emotions of fear, doubt, and worry. If a large dog has chased you or you have given a speech in front of a big crowd, then you have felt the emotional effects of fear, doubt, and worry surging through your body. That is your amygdala sending chemicals into your body to initiate your fight, flight, or freeze response.

According to Dr. Harold Bafitis,[3] the amygdala cannot fire when you are in a state of gratitude. Being grateful by finding opportunities instead of living out of obligation eliminates fear, doubt, and worry from our lives. Gratitude isn't just some fluffy topic meant to make you feel good for a short period of time. Gratitude is a natural drug to combat negative emotions, and the best part is, it comes without any negative side effects. If you discipline yourself in gratitude, you will physiologically change the way your body functions. To discipline yourself in gratitude, you must develop simple practices to remind yourself to be appreciative every day.

Before I share these practices, I want to remind you that discipline is never easy at first. It takes consistent effort for you to incorporate these practices. It will feel odd at first; you might even feel like you're faking it. But it's worth your effort. As a mentor of mine would say, "Discipline weighs ounces and regret weighs tons." You will never regret the decision to be disciplined, especially once you've gained the associated rewards.

Suggestions for engaging gratitude:

- Gratitude journaling: Write down a few things you're grateful for each day. It could be as simple as a beautiful sunrise or a kind gesture from a friend.
- Gratitude meditation: Spend a few minutes each day focusing on the things you're thankful for. Reflect on the positive aspects of your life.
- Gratitude walks: Take a walk outdoors and pay attention to the things you're grateful for in nature—the sights, sounds, and sensations.
- Gratitude letters: Write a letter (or e-mail or text) expressing your gratitude to someone who has had a positive impact on your life. You can choose to send it or keep it for yourself.

- Gratitude jar: Keep a jar for pieces of paper on which you have written down moments of gratitude. Read them all at the end of the year.
- Gratitude rituals: Create small rituals around gratitude, like saying thanks before meals or before going to bed.
- Daily gratitude challenge: Challenge yourself to find something new to be grateful for each day. It could be something you might have taken for granted.
- Gratitude art or creativity: Express your gratitude through art, writing, music, or another creative outlet you enjoy.
- Gratitude sharing: Share moments of gratitude with friends or family. It can create a positive ripple effect.
- Gratitude app: Use a gratitude app to help track your daily moments of thankfulness.

The key is consistency. Engaging in these practices regularly can help cultivate a more grateful and positive mindset. Be grateful—every day.

A—Adopt One Person Per Day to Encourage

Studies have shown that even single words and phrases like no, shut up, peace, and love create chemical changes in our brains. Through practice, our brain becomes habitual in associating words with certain emotions; even a noncontextual uttering of those words can elicit emotional responses. Imagine the impact of a full-blown negative conversation.

Negative words and expressions affect our primary emotions and unlock our survival/stress response. They increase the flow of cortisol in our bloodstream, leading to a narrowing of focus and restlessness. If those feelings are not mitigated, or a person is exposed to them over and over again, excess cortisol can erode our cognitive capacities and curb our creativity, attention, and motivation.

Positive words, on the other hand, unlock the reward circuit and have rejuvenating effects on the listener. They light up the prefrontal cortex of our brain, an area associated with creativity and cognitive functions such as thinking, memorizing, and information processing. More importantly, positive words and attitudes boost the production of dopamine, thereby increasing our motivation and renewing our focus on the work at hand.

A favorite saying: "They who refresh others will themselves be refreshed." Encouragement is supplementing others with courage, and as you do, you get the supplements as well. Intentionally making it a point to adopt one person per day to encourage will develop your strength and your clarity of expression, making you less vulnerable and more connected. Most people do not receive much encouragement, and when encouraged are either elated or disbelieve what was said. Regardless, encouragement changes people's disposition and helps them see themselves from an elevated state of mind.

Suggestions for adopting one person per day:

- Offer genuine compliments to brighten someone's day. Acknowledge their efforts and achievements.
- Listen attentively when someone talks to you. Show that you care about their thoughts and feelings.
- Share positive affirmations or words of encouragement with friends, family, or colleagues.
- Send a thoughtful text or message to check in on someone and let them know you're there for them.
- Recognize and celebrate even small victories and milestones in others' lives or work.
- Perform random acts of kindness, like helping with tasks or surprising someone with a small gift.
- Ask if there's any way you can assist or help someone, especially when they're facing challenges.
- Offer guidance and mentorship to someone who may benefit from your knowledge or experience.
- Share motivational quotes, articles, or videos that resonate with you and could inspire others.
- Remind people to take care of themselves physically and mentally. Encourage them to prioritize self-care.
- Let people know you appreciate their presence in your life and the positive impact they have on you.

- When appropriate, offer constructive feedback without being critical.
- Act as a cheerleader for someone's goals and dreams, offering encouragement and support.
- Show empathy by understanding and validating someone's feelings, especially during difficult times.
- Be there for someone in a time of need, whether it's offering a shoulder to lean on or sharing their joys.

Remember that small acts of encouragement can have a significant impact on someone's day and overall well-being. But for you, the benefits are endless. Encouraging others helps you see them in a positive light, helps you connect with people at deeper levels, and boosts your problem-solving creativity. Additionally, when you are sincere, people will be more comfortable approaching you when they face challenges.

I encourage you to follow Dale Carnegie's advice from his famous work *How to Win Friends and Influence People*, "Be hearty in approbation and lavish in your praise."

D—Determine Priorities Through the PVD Planning Tool: At high performance, we developed the PVD planning tool by combining our PVD system with the Eisenhower Matrix (also known as the Urgent-Important Matrix), a simple yet effective way to prioritize tasks and make decisions about how to allocate your time and effort. The matrix was popularized by President Dwight D. Eisenhower, who was also a five-star general in the U.S. Army and known for his ability to manage time and tasks effectively. Statistically, it is the most effective prioritization tool ever developed.

The matrix categorizes tasks into four quadrants based on two key criteria: urgency and importance:

- Quadrant I: urgent and important
  - Tasks that require immediate attention and are critically important;
  - Tasks often associated with deadlines, crises, and emergencies;
  - Focus on these tasks as a top priority.

- Quadrant II: not urgent but important
  - Tasks that are important for your long-term goals and well-being;
  - Tasks that might not have immediate deadlines but contribute significantly to your success and happiness;
  - Schedule time to focus on these tasks to prevent them from becoming urgent.
- Quadrant III: urgent but not important
  - Tasks that seem pressing but don't contribute much to your long-term goals or values;
  - Tasks that involve distractions, interruptions, or other people's priorities;
  - Try to delegate or minimize the time you spend on these tasks.
- Quadrant IV: not urgent and not important
  - Tasks that are neither pressing nor valuable to your goals or well-being;
  - Tasks that are typically timewasters and distractions;
  - Consider eliminating or minimizing activities related to these tasks to free up time for Quadrant II tasks.

The key to effective prioritization using the Eisenhower Matrix is to focus your energy and time on Quadrants I and II, to address immediate needs while also investing in activities that align with your long-term goals and values. By reducing time spent on Quadrants III and IV, you can increase your productivity and overall satisfaction. Regularly reviewing and updating your task list using this model can help you make better decisions about how to allocate your resources and achieve a balance between short-term demands and long-term priorities.

Too many leaders spend too much time in Quadrants III and IV. This is not because they don't understand priorities, but because they have not set clear expectations, given clear responsibilities, or put measures of accountability in place. Additionally, many leaders have not taught their teams how to prioritize their own days. These are simple fixes, but before teaching others, leaders need to be consistent in living them themselves.

PVD *for Activities and Connections*

Every activity we engage in is a task or connection, or both. PVD—purpose, vision, and discipline—is as relevant for current activities as it is for broader, long-term planning. When planning your days, you want to ensure that every activity is filtered through PVD. For example:

Activity: Review nine contracts to ensure accuracy in the scope of work and that profit margins align with our financial goals.

A task or connection? Task.

- What is the *purpose* of this activity?
  - ○ To ensure what the client wants is clearly communicated in context.
  - ○ To ensure a win-win scenario for client and organization.
- What is our *vision* for this activity?
  - ○ To eliminate any mistakes in the documents.
  - ○ To complete the task within 24 hours.
  - ○ To impress our clients with clarity and professionalism.
- What are the *disciplines* needed to complete this activity?
  - ○ 10 minutes of dedicated time for each contract.
  - ○ Focus: Eliminate distractions and set a 10-minute timer to increase urgency and competitiveness.
- Priority level: Quadrant II. To be completed within four business days.
- Action steps: Schedule 30 minutes per day for three business days; spend 10 minutes each on 3 reviews each day and finish a day before the deadline.

The PVD planning tool will help you be intentional in ensuring that what you are doing is a top-tier priority and that the PVD of each activity is clear. Additionally, the tool will ensure that your action steps are also mapped out.

Completing your PVD planning tool should take roughly 15 minutes per day. Some people do it while they're doing the L, E, and A sections of the LEAD Your Day process. Others do it at night before bed and then briefly review it before engaging in the workday. Others do it when they arrive at work. Find out what works for you and be consistent with it, because by spending minutes developing priorities and planning, you will spend significantly less time in chaos and more time in alpha brainwaves where you can think macro and solve higher-level problems at scale.

Additional Self-Leadership Disciplines

The PVD planning tool is excellent for providing consistency, clarity, and intentionality. Once you have mastered it, you can integrate additional self-leadership disciplines into your life.

- *Proactive care for your body and mind:* Great leaders understand that leadership is holistic and they need to be healthy in mind, body, and spirit. In the world of nutrition and exercise, while there are many eating plans and exercise routines that work, there is no one-size-fits-all. Still, one thing we know unequivocally is that body care is important. The challenges we face as leaders will exhaust our body, mind, and spirit. Each must be in tip-top shape to face challenges and be an effective leader. I highly recommend that you meet with a nutritionist and a personal trainer who can assess you and help you build a routine based on those assessments. In the meantime, here are a few considerations when searching for eating and exercise routines.
- *Nutrition:* One of the most important nutrition considerations is balance, getting the right proportions of macronutrients (carbohydrates, proteins, and fats) and micronutrients (vitamins and minerals) to support your overall health. A balanced eating routine supports not only physical health but also mental well-being. Nutrient-rich foods can positively impact mood and cognitive function.
- *Exercise:* Exercise should be enjoyable and sustainable. Finding activities you like and can stick with makes it more likely that you'll maintain a consistent exercise routine over time. Consulting with a fitness expert or personal trainer can also

help you design a workout plan tailored to your needs and goals.

- *Mind care:* Our minds are like thought factories and we are the plant managers. To have the type of production in our lives that we want, we must be intentional in feeding our minds the right material. And we must be vigilant in reducing the negative thoughts that come into our minds. Remember the short saying, "What you think, is what you feel, is what you do."

- *Academic-based leadership material:* To be a great leader, you must consistently feed your mind positive, academic-based leadership material and reduce the amount of negative material you are consuming, such as the news, conversations that are filled with BCDE, and other noise that leads to negative thinking. Research and other academic-based leadership materials are distinctly different from leadership content authored by nonacademic business leaders. Academic research offers a rigorous and evidence-based approach to leadership, grounded in scientific methodologies and peer-reviewed studies, ensuring that the information is not solely reliant on personal anecdotes or biases but is rooted in empirical data and validated theories. Academic work encourages critical thinking and a deeper understanding of leadership concepts, providing a solid foundation for effective leadership practices. It also evolves with time as new research emerges, allowing leaders to stay updated with the latest insights. Conversely, while nonacademic business leaders can offer valuable practical experiences and anecdotes, their perspectives may be subjective and not universally applicable. Academic-based leadership material complements practical insights, fostering a more holistic and well-informed approach to leadership development and decision making.

A selection of academic-based leadership books that are highly regarded and recommended for leaders:

- *Leadership in Organizations* by Gary Yukl: a comprehensive text providing a solid foundation in leadership theories and research.
- *Leadership: Theory and Practice* by Peter G. Northouse: a widely used textbook exploring various leadership models and their applications.
- *The Leadership Challenge* by James M. Kouzes and Barry Z. Posner: an outline of five key practices of exemplary leadership based on extensive research.
- *Primal Leadership* by Daniel Goleman, Richard E. Boyatzis, and Annie McKee: a deep dive into emotional intelligence and its impact on effective leadership.
- *Good to Great* by Jim Collins: not solely focused on leadership but offering valuable insights into leadership qualities that drive organizational success.
- *Drive: The Surprising Truth About What Motivates Us* by Daniel H. Pink: exploring motivation and how it relates to leadership and productivity, drawing from research in psychology and behavioral economics.
- *Leadership and Self-Deception* by The Arbinger Institute: a unique perspective on leadership through the lens of self-awareness and interpersonal relationships.
- *Leadership BS: Fixing Workplaces and Careers One Truth at a Time* by Jeffrey Pfeffer: challenging conventional leadership wisdom with data-driven insights.
- *Mindset: The New Psychology of Success* by Carol S. Dweck: primarily about personal growth with implications for leadership through discussion of the growth versus fixed mindset concept.

These texts cover a range of leadership topics, from theories and models to practical applications and personal development. Depending on your interests and needs as a leader, you will likely find some more relevant than others.

If you learn better through auditory stimulation, here are some academic-based leadership podcasts that provide valuable insights into leadership theories and practices:

- *The Darden School of Business Podcast*: produced by the University of Virginia's Darden School of Business and featuring academic discussions on leadership, management, and business strategy.
- *The Leadership Podcast*: hosted by two former Navy SEALs and combining practical leadership insights with research-based perspectives, making it both informative and actionable.
- *The Knowledge Project with Shane Parrish*: not exclusively focused on leadership but exploring decision making, cognitive biases, and other topics highly relevant to effective leadership.
- *The McKinsey Podcast*: produced by McKinsey & Company, a global management consulting firm and covering various leadership and business-related topics with insights from experts.
- *The Harvard Business Review IdeaCast*: featuring interviews with leading management and leadership researchers, discussing their latest findings.
- *Leadership and Loyalty Podcast*: hosted by Dov Baron and exploring leadership psychology through interviews with experts in the field.
- *The Engaging Leader Podcast*: hosted by Jesse Lahey, this podcast combines leadership research and practical tips for engaging leadership in organizations.
- *The Coaching for Leaders Podcast*: centered around leadership and coaching and including interviews with academic experts who share insights on leadership development.
- *The NeuroLeadership Podcast*: focused on the intersection of neuroscience and leadership; exploring how the brain impacts leadership behaviors and decision making.

- *The Simon Sinek Podcast*: hosted by Simon Sinek, known for his insights on leadership and purpose, with frequent discussions of academic research and its applications in leadership and business.

These podcasts offer a mix of academic research, practical leadership advice, and real-world insights, making them valuable resources for leaders seeking to enhance their knowledge and skills.

Practice, Practice, Practice

It is the application of our education that makes the biggest difference in our lives. We learn in two ways: through repetitive auditory and visual stimulations and through intense emotional experiences. We learn five times more through intense emotional experiences, which reminds us to take immediate action on ideas that compel us. Too often, leaders want to have a perfect plan in place before they practice what they learn. But you can't have a perfect plan until you have the right practices, which only come through trying, failing, and correcting your course. Each time we practice, we learn and grow, and as long as we keep practicing, failures eventually turn into successes.

I recommend that every day, you practice at least one thing you've learned. You may practice the same discipline every day for a while until you perfect it and move on to the next discipline. Or you may be more abstract and practice a bevy of new disciplines at once. How you do it is up to you, but you must practice. And disregard the old platitude, "Practice makes perfect." The goal is to master daily disciplines, but the aim is not perfection; it's progress.

Evangelist Robert Schuler said, "Spectacular achievements are always preceded by unspectacular preparation." You will not be intentional in leadership if you do not LEAD Your Day intentionally. If you haven't been intentional, start now. Use the LEAD system to lead tomorrow. And once you are using it consistently, pass it on to your team. Teach them to set goals, be intentional, and take immediate action. It is one of the greatest gifts you can give your team. We'll discuss just how to do that effectively in the final part of **The Leadership Edge**, *Building Team Cohesiveness by Building Effective Relationships.*

Your greatest leadership challenge is and always will be self-leadership. If you lead yourself, stay humble, and always look to improve and grow; leading others will be easier because a big part of leading others is teaching them to lead themselves, and you cannot do that well unless you lead yourself well.

Chapter 8 Takeaways

- Leadership without discipline is dangerous. Discipline sustains leadership.
- Listening to yourself is a great gift, not only to yourself but to those you lead. Listening allows you the chance to engage your critical thinking skills, which is your leadership problem-solving funnel.
- The Eisenhower Matrix is a simple yet effective way to prioritize tasks and make decisions about how to allocate your time and effort. It is the most effective prioritization tool ever developed.
- Every activity we engage in is a task or connection, or both. PVD—purpose, vision, and discipline—is as relevant for current activities as it is for broader, long-term planning.
- It is the application of our education that makes the biggest difference in our lives.

PART 3

Building a Culture of Leadership Development

CHAPTER 9

Leading a Powerful Culture

In late 2001, I faced one of the most frightening and beautiful moments of my life. I was in the Middle East, a sailor in the U.S. Navy's Seventh Fleet aboard the USS Kitty Hawk. We carried more than 600 special forces personnel on a special mission to locate and attack terrorists on all fronts. The mission made us a target for counterattacks at any time.

We had landed in the Middle East just weeks after the 9/11 attacks on the World Trade Center and were drilling three or four times a day, at all hours, day and night, in preparation for any and every scenario: fire, flood, mines, biological warfare, missile hits, 50-caliber gunfire, and more. We were intentional about every process, action, and communication as we prepared. When drills were announced over the loudspeaker, an alarm bell would ring, followed by the announcement, "General Quarters, General Quarters, man your battle stations. This is a drill. I repeat, this is a drill." After that announcement, there was relief knowing we weren't under live attack and we could calmly and deliberately complete the drill.

Then, in the middle of a calm night, the alarm bell rang over the loudspeakers, "General Quarters, General Quarters, man your battle stations. This is not a drill. I repeat, this is not a drill." Not a drill, but in fact, very real: We were under threat of attack. Instantly, fear gripped me, and a tingling sensation surged from the bottom of my feet to the top of my head. I felt like I was in a fog, but I knew others were counting on me and that if I didn't do my part, lives could be lost. My body seemed to carry me toward my battle station, and as it did, I saw one of the most beautiful things I have ever seen: trust. Men and women from all walks of life, from different ethnic, religious, and social backgrounds, trusting each other to maintain our mission, to act as one toward a common purpose, vision, and with symbiotic disciplines. We were unified in mind, body, and essence. We moved with urgency but not haste. We communicated abundantly but with few words. We were bold but careful. We were serious but relaxed. And in the end, we were successful in extinguishing the threat.

After we received the order to stand down, there was a collective sigh of relief. Soldiers and sailors hugged, laughed, and cried. We celebrated and debriefed, then went right back to drilling in preparation for another attack. We never lost sight of fulfilling our purpose, vision, and discipline. That was our way of life. That was our culture. It was powerful and unified, and we performed at the highest level.

But it didn't begin that way.

Just a year before, I had arrived at boot camp with hundreds of men and women from different states, counties, and countries. We had different ethnic, religious, educational, and socioeconomic backgrounds. None of us knew how to be a contributing member of the U.S. armed forces. We didn't know how to think, behave, or communicate as one. We didn't trust each other, and we were selfish, undisciplined, and purposeless. Each of us had joined the military for a different reason; the only things in common were our desire to improve our lives and our trust in the military to help us do that.

In boot camp, we were trained how to set our vision and goals and to think with a growth mindset. We were trained how to behave in a way that contributed to improving the quality of life of those around us, and we were taught how to communicate with intentionality, clarity, and authority. Everything we learned was intentionally designed around the mindset of service before self. We were challenged, stretched, and pushed to our limits. Sometimes, it felt like we couldn't take another day, another drill, or sit through another class. But every time we overcame adversity, it strengthened our belief that together we were limitless, together we had a purpose, together we could achieve more.

Companies and Clients

When I was discharged from the Navy and entered the corporate world as an account executive at an information technology (IT) firm, I expected to find organizational structure, training, and intentionality similar to what I experienced in the military. But that was not my experience, both at my firm and with many of our clients. Going from a unified, systematic, and ownership-driven culture to working with so many organizations that lacked intentionality, solid systems, and trust was troubling. Not that the military was perfect; we made our share of mistakes. But the majority of the time, our mistakes were from missing our mark, not from not having a mark to aim at.

My client meetings typically started with two questions:

1. What do you want for your IT ecosystem?
2. What roadblocks are keeping you from what you want?

I was astonished at how often clients would respond, "I don't know" or "I need to think about it" to question one. But I was more astonished at how often they'd site people, team members, as well as clients in answering question 2. They would say things like "People don't follow the systems," "People aren't held accountable," and "People complain and call the help desk about things we've already instructed them on."

More answers centered around people being noncompliant, or staunchly resistant to change, especially changes in technology. At that time, I was studying to complete my graduate degree in Organizational Leadership. My thesis topic was "leading a powerful organizational culture," and I'd studied enough—and had experienced enough—to give my clients ideas on how to get buy-in and compliance from their organizations.

Over time I was not only consulting on IT but also on leadership. And when I spoke with leaders about organizational culture, while many understood its importance, few had the knowledge or skills to build a powerful culture in their organization.

What Is Culture?

The formal definition of culture is "the customs, beliefs, values, norms, and standards of a people group." More precisely, culture is your organization's way of life. It is built on your habits, those subconscious acts that account for 95 percent of your life. As such, the way an organization's people think, feel, work, communicate, react, plan, and behave is overwhelmingly influenced by habit. Your habits determine your results; your results inform you of whether or not you have good habits. And if you want better, sustainable results for your business, your employees, and yourself, you and your team must be intentional about building your culture on the right habits, sustaining them, and improving them as your organization grows.

Powerful cultures are the result of powerful choices. The complexity and simplicity of being human are in our ability to choose to think, behave, and communicate in any way we want. Those choices produce results, and if we're not intentional about thinking through the results we want and making choices that are aligned with those desired results, we will have to live with the consequences of being unintentional.

It is our ability to choose how we think, behave, and communicate that makes us free and powerful. Powerful leaders build cultures where people have the ability to make choices about values, systems, behaviors, and communication practices that will contribute to their organization's successes or failures, and the right or duty to take responsibility for their part in both. Weak leaders attempt to take choices away from their people in an attempt to control behavior and outcomes. But those attempts ultimately fall short because people will not allow themselves to be controlled over prolonged periods of time.

To be powerful, leaders must shift from a "command and control" mindset where all responsibility falls on the leader to an "empowerment and accountability" mindset where responsibilities are shared, even if the ultimate responsibility still falls on the leader. This is risky because people make bad choices sometimes. They can be rude, thoughtless, inconsiderate, selfish, haphazard, and lazy, which makes the command-and-control style of leadership appealing to so many. But a culture of empowerment and accountability can create rewards beyond measure because people can be ingenious, kind, disciplined, principled, and responsible, and perhaps most importantly, can choose to change for the better. And when people become habituated to making choices that are in their and their organization's best interests, the organization grows and thrives.

When I was in the military, I was empowered with responsibilities. I was given the tools, skills, and support to lead myself and others. And I was relationally and systematically held accountable for my choices and results. Being in that culture nurtured creative thought, communication skills, efficacy, relational connections, and a deep sense of belonging and purpose. In my consulting practice, I've worked with clients who have allowed me to help them create the same environment for their team members, and many have experienced similar results.

To build a powerful culture, leaders must create a collaborative as well as accountable environment. I've worked with many leaders who tried to build a powerful culture on their own. Many came up with brilliant ideas and strategies, but implementation failed because it was *their* brilliant ideas and strategies, not their team's. Too often a leader is portrayed in pop culture as the person with all the answers, all the power, all the intelligence. But the best leaders are those who elevate others. As summed up by Mahatma Gandhi, "Leaders aren't measured by how many followers they have, but by how many leaders they create."

You, as a leader, can choose how you want to lead. But I assure you that I've never seen an organization enjoy sustained success under command-and-control leadership. I have, however, seen success beyond expectation in powerful cultures where empowerment and accountability are the norm. I've seen a company that was nearly bankrupt grow from $10 million in sales to more than $100 million in six years. I've seen an organization go from a more than 50 percent turnover rate to a 92 percent retention rate. I've seen a business go from a reputation for being a bad place to work to being named "business of the year" by their community.

In the remaining chapters of *The Leadership Edge*, I will detail the structure, systems, and disciplines that leaders use to build and lead powerful cultures where people are empowered to make choices and held accountable for those choices. While self-leadership is fundamental to leading, building and leading powerful cultures is how to grow and scale a business.

Chapter 9 Takeaways

- The way an organization's people think, feel, work, communicate, react, plan, and behave is overwhelmingly influenced by habit.

- Powerful leaders build cultures where people have the ability to make choices about values, systems, behaviors, and communication practices that will contribute to their organization's successes or failures.
- To build a powerful culture, leaders must create a collaborative as well as accountable environment.
- The best leaders are those who elevate others.
- While self-leadership is fundamental to leading, building and leading powerful cultures is how to grow and scale a business.

CHAPTER 10

Building the Structure of a Powerful Culture

One of the most impressive cultural changes I've ever witnessed was at A Plus Powder Coaters of Columbiana, Ohio. When I first met with A Plus Founder and Owner Bob Bertelsen, he had been attempting to motivate people mostly through extrinsic rewards, which included bonuses, a points system for attendance, a generous health care program, and financial literacy programs. But his people were still trying to beat the company's system by doing just enough not to compromise their jobs. The final straw for Bob was when an employee called in to ask how many attendance points he had remaining and promptly took the day off once he knew he was safe from being written up. That day, Bob called me and asked if we could meet.

Bob Bertelsen is an exceptional leader. If he believes something needs to change, he changes it. He doesn't hesitate. He makes decisions, evaluates the results, and if they aren't what he expects, tries another approach. The successes at A Plus have been the direct result of his and his team's leadership. My involvement in the process was as a facilitator and guide; I take no credit for their success. Powerful cultures can only be established where there are powerful leaders. And Bob is unquestionably a powerful leader.

A few days later, I sat with Bob and his COO, Terry Watson, in the A Plus conference room, listening to their frustrations over their teams' seeming disinterest and selfishness. They explained in detail their company's structure and how their culture was built. I could tell they were putting a great deal of time, energy, and effort into it. I asked them if they'd ever considered including their team in structuring their culture. They hadn't. I went on to explain how including their team would make every team member an owner of the culture, and their behavior would change accordingly.

We decided to conduct a cultural remodel, where we would share the company's vision and include the team in remodeling the structure of the company's mission, values, and accountability standards that would be followed to reach the vision. Over the following months, we met once weekly with the entire A Plus team and were successful in establishing a new mission statement, values, and standards of accountability as follows:

A Plus mission: Be our best for everyone's success.

A Plus values:

- ° Respect: We will be respectful and honest with co-workers, customers, and ourselves.
- ° Attitude: We will find positive solutions, and we won't accept negative behavior.
- ° Quality: We will do things the right way.

A Plus Accountability Our accountability structures and systems will remind each other of our values and commitment to the mission and vision. For example, when someone exhibited a poor attitude, we sent them, in a kind way, to another room to "check their attitude." This was to remind them of the importance of a positive attitude to creating real solutions for our customers and good relationships among our team members. We discussed various methods for creating accountability standards for each value, and once they were established, everyone committed, then agreed to meet monthly to conduct a culture assessment to evaluate how we were doing and to discuss one of the values, the mission, or another professional development topic.

Once everyone agreed to the changes, they went to work implementing them. The results were beyond expectations. Roughly a year and a half later, A Plus was facing a downturn in their business and in danger of having to lay people off. Instead of trying to create solutions on his own, Bob shared the difficult news with his team and asked them to think of possible solutions. A few days later, a handful of team members approached Bob with an idea: Reduce everyone's hours, and all would share the pain as opposed to laying off team members with less seniority. Bob was proud of his team for their suggestion, but instead of implementing it right away, he asked everyone to vote on it at their next monthly culture meeting. And the vote was unanimous: They'd sacrifice their hours to save everyone's job.

The cultural remodel worked. A Plus was walking the talk. They went from being careless to taking care of one another, from being selfish to selfless, doing just enough to get by to doing far more than what was expected. Over the past 10 years, A Plus has tripled its revenues. They have the highest quality ratings in the manufacturing industry. And they are a preferred employer in their region. Best of all, the team members at A Plus have built lifelong relationships with one another structured on values and belonging and contributing to a purpose bigger than self.

The A Plus Powder Coaters business culture is a testament to the vital importance of leaders establishing a strong cultural structure where everyone is empowered to choose their way of life.

Having a solid business structure is essential for effective leadership for three reasons:

1. It provides a clear hierarchy and delineation of responsibilities, ensuring that each team member knows their role and whom to report to. Too often there is confusion about who is responsible for specific tasks, connections, and deadlines. Structural clarity reduces confusion and minimizes conflicts, enabling leaders to focus on strategic decisions rather than correcting internal disputes.
2. A well-defined structure fosters accountability as individuals understand their performance expectations and who they report to and why. It allows them to take ownership of their tasks and meet deadlines.
3. It facilitates efficient communication channels, allowing leaders to disseminate information swiftly and gather feedback effectively.

Furthermore, a sound structure supports scalability, as the organization can adapt and grow without experiencing chaos or inefficiencies. In essence, a good business structure serves as the backbone of effective leadership, promoting order, accountability, and agility within the organization.

Let's now examine three types of structures: culture, assessment, and relationship.

Culture Structure

Edgar Schein,[1] a renowned organizational psychologist, developed a model that structures organizational culture into three levels of depth, each with its own characteristics:

1. *Level 1: Artifacts and behaviors (surface level):* Artifacts are the visible and tangible elements that represent a group's customs, values, and shared behaviors. These can include things like clothing styles, office layouts, symbols, rituals, and everyday practices that are observable within a particular culture. Artifacts serve as outward expressions of deeper cultural values and assumptions, offering clues to an organization's identity and norms. They provide a surface-level glimpse into the culture's character and can be a valuable starting point for understanding it. However, it's essential to recognize that while artifacts are readily observable, they might not always reveal the complete picture of an organization's culture, as they often only scratch the surface of the more profound, underlying beliefs and values that shape the culture.

For example, you might observe the following artifacts in the office décor and layout of a business with a culture that values collaboration, innovation, open communication, and a relaxed work environment:

- Open office layout: The physical workspace is designed with minimal barriers, featuring an open floor plan with shared workstations or collaborative areas. The layout encourages employees to interact freely and exchange ideas.
- Inspirational wall art: Throughout the office, you find motivational quotes, images, and artwork that reflect the company's values and vision. These visuals serve as reminders of the organization's culture and goals.

- Casual dress code: Employees often dress informally, such as in jeans and t-shirts, rather than formal business attire. This dress code signals a culture that prioritizes comfort and a relaxed atmosphere.
- Team meeting spaces: Meeting rooms are equipped with whiteboards, comfortable seating, and technology for group discussions and brainstorming sessions. This indicates a culture that values teamwork and collaborative problem-solving.
- Recreational areas: The office has areas with games like foosball and ping pong or a lounge with comfortable seating. These spaces promote breaks, relaxation, and social interaction, fostering a culture of work-life balance and employee well-being.

Such artifacts collectively convey the cultural values and priorities of the organization. But while artifacts provide insights into culture, they should be considered alongside espoused values and deeper assumptions for a more comprehensive understanding of the organization's culture.

2. *Level 2: Espoused values and beliefs (intermediate level):* Espoused beliefs and values in a culture refer to the explicit and stated principles, philosophies, and ideals that an organization or group claims to uphold. These are the articulated norms and standards that are officially communicated to employees, customers, and stakeholders. Espoused beliefs and values are often found in the company's purpose, vision, and core value declarations that inform a company's disciplines. They represent the aspirational aspects of an organization's culture and serve as a guide for decision making and behavior. However, while these values are openly expressed, they might not always align perfectly with the actual behaviors and practices observed within the culture. Understanding espoused beliefs and values is essential for assessing an organization's stated commitments and comparing them to the reality of its cultural practices and behaviors, as identified in artifacts and deeper assumptions.

Imagine a retail company that espouses a strong commitment to being customer-centric. Some ways this might manifest in the organization's culture:

- Customer-centric purpose: The company's purpose is explicit in its dedication to delivering exceptional customer experiences, putting the customer at the center of everything it does.
- Customer feedback initiatives: The organization actively seeks and values customer feedback, using it to make improvements and adjustments to products, services, and processes.
- Employee training: Employees receive extensive training focused on customer service, empathy, and effective communication to ensure they align with the company's customer-centric values.
- Performance metrics: Employee performance evaluations and rewards are tied to customer satisfaction scores and feedback, reinforcing the importance of meeting customer needs.
- Flexibility to solve problems: Employees are empowered to make decisions that benefit the customer, even if it means going beyond standard policies or procedures.
- Product development: When developing new products or services, the organization prioritizes features and improvements based on customer needs and preferences.

In this example, the company's espoused beliefs and values are centered around prioritizing the customer. These values are not only articulated but also integrated into various aspects of the company's operations, from its purpose to employee training and decision making. This demonstrates a commitment to aligning culture with the stated values, creating a customer-centric environment throughout the organization. However, it's crucial to ensure that these espoused values are consistently upheld and reflected in actual behaviors and practices to maintain a truly customer-centric culture.

3. *Level 3: Basic assumptions and unconscious beliefs (deep level):* Basic assumptions and unconscious beliefs in a culture are the deepest yet

often unspoken elements that underlie and shape an organization's values, behaviors, and decision-making processes. These assumptions are so ingrained in the culture that they are taken for granted and rarely questioned by members of the organization. They represent the core, foundational beliefs that influence how individuals perceive the world, interact with others, and make sense of their environment. These assumptions are typically implicit and not explicitly articulated, making them challenging to identify and change. They form the cultural "norms" that guide behavior, and they are essential for understanding why people within a culture act the way they do, even when those actions may seem illogical or contrary to stated values. Uncovering and addressing these basic assumptions is crucial for deep cultural transformation and aligning the culture with desired values and goals.

Consider, for example, a business culture where there's a strong fear of failure. Basic assumptions and unconscious beliefs may manifest themselves as follows:

- Decision avoidance: Employees might avoid making decisions, especially those with potential risks because they fear negative consequences like reprimands or job insecurity. This behavior reflects the deep-seated belief that any failure is unacceptable.
- Blame culture: When something goes wrong, there's a tendency to blame individuals rather than examine systemic issues. This reflects an underlying belief that individuals are solely responsible for success or failure.
- Lack of innovation: The organization may struggle to innovate because employees are reluctant to propose new ideas or take creative risks. The core belief is that experimentation is discouraged because it might lead to failure.
- Micromanagement: Managers may micromanage their teams, wanting to maintain tight control over processes and decisions. This stems from a belief that close supervision is necessary to prevent mistakes.

- Conservatism in strategy: The company may stick to traditional, low-risk strategies even in dynamic markets, missing out on opportunities for growth. This is rooted in the belief that safe, well-established practices are the only path to success.

In this example, the deep-seated basic assumption is the fear of failure, which influences various aspects of the business culture, from decision making to innovation and risk tolerance. While the espoused values may indicate a desire for growth and innovation, the unconscious belief in avoiding failure at all costs significantly impacts how employees behave and the organization's overall performance. Identifying and addressing such deep-seated beliefs is essential for cultural transformation to align with desired values and goals.

In essence, Schein's premise was that a holistic understanding of culture requires exploring not only what is visible and stated but also what is deeply ingrained and often hidden from view. By recognizing and addressing all three levels of culture, organizations can better navigate cultural challenges, align their culture with their mission and goals, and drive positive change.

Assessment Structure

Maintaining an ongoing assessment structure for your culture enables adaptability, ensuring your culture evolves with changing times and remains aligned with organizational objectives. Assessments reveal employee engagement, allowing you to address concerns and nurture positivity. Conflict resolution benefits from early detection of issues, promoting a healthier environment. It ensures your culture stays in sync with your core values and purpose, preventing drift. Moreover, ongoing assessments attract and retain talent, enhance performance, and provide a competitive edge. They also help with compliance and ethical standards, making it an essential strategy for a thriving, resilient organization.

Assessing all three levels of your culture provides a holistic view of your organization, helping you ensure alignment between surface-level practices, stated values, and your fundamental, underlying beliefs. Such a comprehensive understanding empowers you to create a culture that supports your mission, engages employees, and promotes a positive and productive work environment.

Some steps you can take to assess the three levels of your culture.

- Interviews and focus groups:
  - Conduct in-depth, one-on-one interviews with employees at various levels of the organization. Encourage them to share stories and experiences that reflect how they perceive the company's culture and what they believe is taken for granted.
  - Organize focus groups with employees to facilitate open discussions about their experiences and beliefs within the organization. Use open-ended questions to encourage participants to express their thoughts freely.
- *Observational analysis:*
  - Observe how employees interact and make decisions in real-life situations. Look for patterns in behavior and decision making that may be influenced by underlying assumptions.
  - Pay attention to how conflicts are resolved, how resources are allocated, and how promotions or rewards are granted, as these actions often reveal hidden cultural biases.
- *Culture assessments with open-ended questions:*
  - Include open-ended questions in your company's culture surveys. Ask employees to describe what they believe is "just the way things are done" or what values they think guide decision making.
  - Analyze the responses to these open-ended questions to identify recurring themes and common assumptions that may not be apparent in quantitative survey data alone.
- *External cultural audits:*
  - Consider bringing in external consultants or experts in cultural analysis. They can conduct confidential interviews and surveys, providing employees with a safe space to share their beliefs and assumptions without fear of repercussions.

- *Storytelling and narrative analysis:*
  - ○ Encourage employees to share stories or anecdotes about their experiences within the organization. These narratives often contain implicit beliefs and assumptions.
  - ○ Analyze the stories to identify recurring themes and underlying cultural elements that influence behavior and decision making.
- *Leadership reflection and feedback:*
  - ○ Meet with organizational leaders and decision makers to reflect on their own beliefs and assumptions. Ask them to consider how their personal values align with the company's culture and if there are any discrepancies.
  - ○ Encourage leaders to seek feedback from their teams about aspects of the organization's culture as they perceive them.

I highly recommend using outside consultants to help in your assessments for several reasons. First, they offer fresh perspectives untainted by internal biases, ensuring a more accurate evaluation. Second, consultants possess specialized knowledge in cultural analysis and change management, enabling them to conduct thorough assessments, identify areas for improvement, and provide strategic recommendations. Third, they create a confidential environment that encourages honest feedback from employees. Fourth, consultants can benchmark your culture against industry standards, highlighting areas for development. And finally, a consultant's involvement results in a well-informed, actionable plan for cultural transformation, fostering a healthier and more aligned organizational culture that drives positive outcomes and employee engagement.

If you choose not to hire a consultant, you can still use these practical approaches to help you uncover the basic assumptions and unconscious beliefs that shape your company's culture. It's essential to create an environment where employees feel safe sharing their perspectives honestly. Once you have identified these deeper cultural elements, you can work toward aligning them with the espoused values, addressing any discrepancies to create a more cohesive and values-driven organizational culture.

Relationship Structure

Every leadership and organizational success and failure is contingent on the quality, depth, and loyalty of relationships. To repeat a reference from earlier in *The Leadership Edge*, "Relationships are the bridges over which values are transferred." It was one of my dad's favorite sayings; I give him credit for it because he said it so often.

Nothing is more important for a leader than to spend time building strong relationships and providing an environment for strong relationships. Without relationships, teams have no ability to perpetuate the purpose, vision, values, or disciplines of an organization. In strong relationships, we learn about people's dreams, aspirations, and goals. We learn about their purpose for coming to work every day. We learn about their victories and defeats. We learn their preferences, their penchants, and even their vices. But, above all, in strong relationships, people let down their guard and show you who they really are.

When relationships are firmly established, leaders are able to guide, direct, challenge, encourage, and empower their teams through the power of intrinsic motivation toward the fulfillment of their organizations' purpose, vision, and disciplines. Without strong relationships, a leader's effectiveness is diminished; they are unable to tap into the power of intrinsic motivation, allowing for shallow relationships built on the extrinsic motivations of money, prestige, and power.

Building strong relationships begins with structure. Leaders need to adhere to three key principles for structuring effective relationships:

1. Trust and respect: Building trust is crucial. Leaders must be reliable and consistent in their actions and choices. Respect for the expertise and contributions of team members is also vital. Trust and respect form the foundation of a healthy working relationship. Trust is built on common goals, values, and mutual respect. This means leaders have to emphasize that on their team, no one person is more important than the other. Additionally, leaders must connect regularly with each person and ask for feedback both good and bad as a way to create the best environment for success.

2. Communication: Open and transparent communication is essential. Leaders should foster an environment where team members feel comfortable sharing their thoughts and concerns. Leaders must actively listen to their team and provide clear, honest, and constructive feedback. Communication is a key skill for a leader; their level of success will correlate directly with their level of communication. If someone wants to advance, they should focus on their nonverbal, verbal, and written communication. The more proficient a communicator, the more proficient they will be in building strong relationships, powerful cultures, and organizational sustainability.

3. Empowerment and accountability: Leaders must empower their teams by delegating tasks and responsibilities. For a business to grow, scale, thrive, and sustain, leaders must focus on duplicating themselves and working themselves out of a job while, at the same time, looking at the next step in their leadership journey. Powerful leaders encourage their teams to take ownership of their work, and they are quick to give credit for all organizational successes to their teams. Weak leaders are insecure and take the credit for themselves. Powerful leaders also hold team members accountable for their actions and outcomes. This balance of empowerment and accountability fosters growth and responsibility.

These relationship principles form leaders' navigational guidance system. Every encounter, interaction, and self-evaluation should be considered through them. Because they are so important, we will focus on building strong relationships, starting with *trust and respect*, for the remaining chapters of *The Leadership Edge*.

A final note on Chapter 10: Leading a powerful culture starts and ends with a solid structure. Without a sound structure, organizations teeter on the edge of chaos. Leaders must be intentional in ensuring the three levels of culture are aligned. To do this, they should regularly assess their culture and commit to establishing relationships built on common goals, agreed-upon values, and systems of accountability. When they do, they can free themselves from worrying about surviving and focus on taking their business to the next level.

Chapter 10 Takeaways

- It is vitally important for leaders to establish a strong cultural structure where everyone is empowered to choose their way of life.
- A good business structure serves as the backbone of effective leadership, promoting order, accountability, and agility within the organization.
- While artifacts provide insights into culture, they should be considered alongside espoused values and deeper assumptions for a more comprehensive understanding of the organization's culture.
- Basic assumptions and unconscious beliefs in a culture are the deepest yet often unspoken elements that underlie and shape an organization's values, behaviors, and decision-making processes.
- Nothing is more important for a leader than to spend time building strong relationships and providing an environment for strong relationships.
- Powerful leaders encourage their teams to take ownership of their work, and they are quick to give credit for all organizational successes to their teams.

CHAPTER 11

Building Trust and Respect

Mike Krzyzewski, perhaps better known as "Coach K," is widely regarded as one of the greatest college basketball coaches of all time, having built the Duke Blue Devils into a perennial national powerhouse during his tenure. His foundation for success was building trust and respect among his players. As in the fall of 1985, following a season of 23 wins and an appearance in the NCAA tournament, Coach K knew that, with a mix of experienced players and incoming freshmen, the road ahead would be challenging. They needed to mesh together for any chance of another successful season.

One evening, instead of the typical practice, Coach K gathered his team in the gym and had them sit in a circle at center court. He began by speaking about the importance of trust and respect, on and off the court. Then, a team exercise: Each player was to share a personal story, something that had shaped them, whether it was a challenge they overcame, a family memory, or a moment of personal doubt. The only rules were that they had to listen to each story without interrupting, and the stories couldn't be shared outside the circle.

One by one, players began to open up. Some talked about personal losses, others about challenges they faced in their hometowns, and some about the pressures of being a student-athlete. As each story unfolded, a bond started to form among the players. They began to see each other not just as teammates but as brothers with shared struggles and dreams. After the last player spoke, Coach K shared his own story. He talked about his time at West Point, the challenges he faced, and how trust and camaraderie were the keys to overcoming adversity.

The impact of that night was profound. Not only did players' trust and respect for each other increase, they began to understand the importance of playing for each other, not just for themselves or their school. They realized that every player had a story, a reason for being there, and a dream they were chasing. That season those players won 37 games and the ACC Championship and were National Championship runners-up.

Throughout his career, Coach K emphasized the importance of trust, respect, and open communication. Sessions like that of the fall of 1985 built a foundation for the many successful seasons to come. The culture he created and cultivated at Duke was not just about winning basketball games but about building character and developing relationships that would last a lifetime.

Trust and respect are the cornerstones of a successful team, be it in sports, business, or any other collaborative endeavor. Trust forms the basis for open and honest communication, creating an environment where team members feel safe sharing their ideas, concerns, and vulnerabilities. It encourages collaboration and ensures that everyone's input is valued, leading to better decision making and problem-solving. Respect involves acknowledging the unique contributions and perspectives of each team member. When team members respect one another, they are more likely to listen actively, appreciate diverse viewpoints, and work cohesively. Where trust and respect are cultivated, individuals are more motivated to give their best effort, feel a sense of belonging, and work to collectively achieve goals. Absent of trust and respect, teams can become fractured, unproductive, and plagued by conflicts, hindering their ability to achieve success and work harmoniously toward a common purpose.

Building Trust

Trust Principle #1 *Practice service before self:* In leadership, trust is firmly established when team members know their leader will do everything in their power to help them succeed, including sacrificing their own successes for the betterment of others. A smart leader is committed to "service before self." It is not a platitude or a motivational tactic. Smart leaders know that service before self is good business and a way to establish trust. Consider the following example.

Stevie opened a small coffee shop that became known for its exceptional coffee and warm, inviting atmosphere. As the shop gained popularity, Stevie realized she could expand. But instead of opening multiple branches herself, she decided to focus on developing others in her organization as leaders, and then expand through like-minded people. Stevie sat down with her most dedicated and passionate employee, Mark, and began to ask him what he wanted for his career. Mark had similar aspirations as Stevie. He wanted to own and build something with other like-minded people. He wanted to make a lot of money and told Stevie he was looking for that opportunity. When Stevie shared her expansion and partnership idea, Mark was all in.

Stevie took Mark under her wing and mentored him in every aspect of running the coffee shop. She shared her knowledge, values, and business acumen. During their mentoring sessions, Stevie continued to motivate Mark by emphasizing that her sole focus was to help him become successful. She was leading with a service-before-self attitude, and it paid off.

With Stevie's guidance and encouragement, Mark soon became the manager of the shop. Under his leadership, the quality of the coffee and the customer experience continued to be excellent. Stevie knew it was time to take the next step in her plan for duplication and scaling, and together, they opened a second coffee shop in a different part of the city. Mark was put in charge of the new branch, applying the skills and principles he had learned from Stevie. The same exceptional coffee and atmosphere were duplicated in the new location.

Over time, Mark trained and mentored his own team, just as Stevie had done for him. They, in turn, helped open additional coffee shops in different neighborhoods. Stevie's vision for duplication and scaling was in full swing, and soon, there were multiple coffee shops across the city, all maintaining the high standards and service-before-self attitude set by Stevie. The brand became known for quality and consistency. It wasn't just about one person's leadership; it was about replicating and scaling a successful model.

Stevie's approach to leadership led to the growth of her business without her having to be present at every location. The power of duplication and scaling in leadership was evident as her vision and values were carried forward by a team of dedicated and well-trained leaders, ensuring the ongoing success of her brand.

Leaders cannot sustain success unless their team sustains success. And success cannot be sustained without trust. To gain and sustain trust, service before self must be genuine. Everything else is coercion or manipulation, and people are very good at sniffing that out. Never forget that service before self is not just a moral standard, it is a smart business practice. The more you serve others, the better team members they will become, which, in turn, will increase production, loyalty, and care, the foundation needed for duplication and scaling. Serve first, and your needs, wants, and desires will be served.

Adopt these three service-before-self practices:

1. Lead by example: Demonstrate a willingness to put the needs of your team and organization ahead of your personal interests. Show your dedication to a strong work ethic to inspire others to follow suit. Be clear in communicating your commitment to putting your team in the best position to succeed.
2. Be an active listener: Take the time to actively listen to your team members' concerns, ideas, and feedback. Show genuine empathy and support for their well-being and professional growth. Address their needs and concerns effectively. Do not merely listen but implement changes as quickly as you can to prove that you're listening.
3. Empower and develop others: Invest in the development of your team by providing opportunities for skill-building, mentorship, and growth. Encourage them to take on challenges and responsibilities, nurturing their potential as future leaders. Be proactive and disciplined in scheduling time with each team member you want to develop.

By consistently employing these practices, you'll promote a culture of selfless service that can lead to a more engaged and motivated team.

Trust Principle #2

Embrace vulnerability: Vulnerability suggests being susceptible to harm, damage, or exploitation. Vulnerability in leadership builds trust, authenticity, and meaningful connections with team members. When leaders are open about their own imperfections and challenges, it creates a safe environment for others to do the same, which in turn encourages open communication, problem-solving, and collaboration. Leaders who embrace vulnerability are better equipped to build resilient teams and inspire growth.

I'll never forget watching my friends and colleagues Dale and Brian Karmie, owners of ForeverLawn, Inc., at their annual dealer conference standing in front of what at that time were about 60 of their dealers and admitting to mistakes they had made as they grew their business. They told stories and laughed as they recalled specific incidents. As they spoke, I watched their dealers' reactions. They were relaxed and engaged, and for the rest of the conference, many dealers opened up about their mistakes as well, and any tension melted like wax under a candle. In the months following that conference, the production and sales numbers noticeably increased, but more importantly, the connections between dealers and the ForeverLawn home office deepened. Trust had been established, and that year, the company broke every sales record on their books.

Vulnerability is often looked at as weakness. Misguided leadership training programs advise people to not show vulnerability. But that can only lead to disconnection, isolation, and silos within an organization. Leaders are humans leading other humans who can be riddled with fear, doubt, and worries. When a person can't express those concerns to their leader, they are pretending to be someone they are not. Success does not exist without challenges, and challenges come with fear, doubt, and worry. Powerful leaders are able to draw out people's fears and help them overcome them. And when people in your organization are allowed to show their vulnerability, the culture becomes a powerful organism that will grow through any challenge, circumstance, or adversity.

Adopt these three vulnerability practices:

1. Share personal stories: Open up about personal experiences, challenges, or moments of self-doubt that have shaped your leadership journey. Sharing relatable stories can humanize you as a leader and make you more approachable.
2. Admit uncertainty: It's okay to admit that you don't have all the answers. Acknowledging uncertainty and seeking input from your team demonstrates humility and a willingness to collaborate on solutions.

3. Encourage feedback: Create a culture where team members feel comfortable providing feedback on your leadership and the organization. Emphasize that their input is valued and that you're open to constructive criticism.

These practices will help you connect with your team on a deeper level and foster an environment of trust and understanding.

Trust Principle #3

Establish team values: Establishing values builds trust by providing a shared moral compass that guides behaviors and decisions. When team members collectively identify and commit to a set of values, it creates a framework for understanding what is expected in terms of behavior, integrity, and priorities. A shared commitment to living a set of values establishes a sense of safety, predictability, and reliability, where team members know they are working toward common goals based on a solid ethical foundation. As teams embody the same values, they become unified in heart, mind, and purpose. And with time and consistent practice, trust is established. Trust is the greatest currency in any relationship. If you're in a relationship with someone who does not share your values, it can be disastrous.

For example, in a fast-paced startup, two partners, Emily and Alex, had contrasting values. Emily prioritized transparency and customer trust. She insisted on delivering quality products, even if it meant delaying launches. Alex, however, valued rapid growth and immediate profits above all. He pushed for speed and was not as concerned with product integrity. Initially, they secured a substantial customer base, but Alex overpromised and underdelivered, and as quality issues emerged, customer trust eroded. Emily's values had led to customer loyalty, referrals, and sustainable growth but Alex's approach backfired and the business incurred costly recalls and a damaged reputation. Worst of all, Emily lost trust in Alex.

Imagine Emily and Alex discussing and deciding on values to guide their relationship and business. Their shared values would have informed their habits and united them in how they thought, behaved, and communicated. Over time, trust would have become an underlying assumption because they would've inherently known, no matter the circumstances, the values that were guiding their thoughts, behaviors, and communication.

When values are established, it enhances collaboration, reduces conflicts, and encourages open communication, ultimately leading to a more cohesive and high-performing team.

Adopt these practices to establish team values:

- Hold collaborative discussions: Engage your team in open and collaborative discussions to identify and define the core values that resonate with everyone. Encourage input from all team members to ensure a collective and inclusive approach. Don't become defensive when you hear challenging feedback; embrace it and focus discussions on how to improve.
- Align your values with purpose and vision: Ensure that the chosen values align with the organization's purpose and vision. Values should support the overarching goals and purpose of the team or company, reinforcing a sense of purpose and direction.
- Reinforce your values: Regularly communicate and reinforce the team values in all aspects of your work. Integrate them into decision making, recognition, and performance evaluations. Consistent reinforcement helps solidify the values as an integral part of the team's culture.

These practices will help you establish values that guide your team's behavior, decisions, and interactions, contributing to a cohesive and aligned group.

Building Respect

Respect Principle #1

Consistency: Being consistent in behavior fosters respect in relationships by creating a sense of predictability and reliability. When individuals consistently act in alignment with their values and commitments, it demonstrates integrity and authenticity. Predictability allows others to know what to expect, which, in turn, reduces uncertainty and anxiety. Furthermore, consistent behavior shows that you respect not only your own principles but also the expectations and needs of those you interact with. As a result, respect flourishes because people understand you as reliable and authentic, the fundamentals of a healthy and trusting relationship. In short, it's what you do, not what you say that builds respect.

Mahatma Gandhi was known for consistency and earning respect. Throughout his life, Gandhi consistently adhered to his principles of nonviolent resistance and civil disobedience in his quest for Indian independence from British colonial rule. His unwavering commitment to nonviolence, even in the face of harsh oppression and violence from the British, earned him immense respect both within India and internationally. He consistently lived a simple life, eschewing material wealth and leading by example, which resonated deeply with the Indian people.

Gandhi's consistency in behavior and principles inspired countless followers to join the Indian independence movement, and his dedication to nonviolence also influenced other civil rights leaders, including Martin Luther King Jr. His determination to remain true to his principles and consistent in his approach not only earned him respect but also played a pivotal role in achieving India's independence, making him a revered figure in history.

Consistency in attitude, effort, and communication shows your team that you embody your beliefs, values, and purpose.

Adopt these three practices of consistency:

1. Communicate clearly: Effective leaders consistently communicate their expectations, vision, and goals to their teams. Clear and transparent communication ensures that everyone understands their roles, responsibilities, and the broader objectives of the organization. Consistency in communication helps avoid misunderstandings, aligns team members, and fosters a shared sense of purpose.

2. Be reliable in decision making: Consistency in decision making is crucial for earning the trust and respect of your team. Leaders should apply a consistent decision-making process, whether it's through

data analysis, consulting with experts, or consideration of the organization's values and goals. Making fair and consistent decisions,
even in challenging situations, demonstrates a steady and depend-
able leadership style.

3. Lead by example: Consistent leaders set a reliable example through
their behavior and work ethic. They adhere to the same standards
and expectations they set for their team. By consistently demon-
strating dedication, professionalism, and a strong work ethic, leaders
inspire their teams to follow suit. Leading by example is a powerful
way to establish a culture of consistency within the organization.

By practicing these key elements of leadership consistently, you can
build trust, reliability, and a strong foundation for your leadership.

Respect Principle #2

Empathy: Empathy is essential for establishing respect in relationships
because it signifies a genuine understanding and concern for the feelings, perspectives, and needs of others. When we express empathy, we
acknowledge the emotions and experiences of those we interact with,
establishing a sense of validation and care. When you recognize and val-
idate peoples' humanity and individuality, you send a powerful message
that their thoughts and feelings matter to you, whether you agree with
them or not. This acknowledgment forms the basis of mutual respect, as it
shows that you value and appreciate the experiences and emotions of others. By empathizing with those around you, you create an environment
where people feel heard, valued, and respected, ultimately strengthening
the bonds of trust and connection in the relationship.

Nelson Mandela was known for earning respect through empathy.
His empathetic leadership played a crucial role in dismantling apartheid
in South Africa. During his 27 years of imprisonment, he never wavered
in his commitment to reconciliation and understanding between races.
Upon his release, he displayed remarkable empathy by working to unite a
deeply divided nation, emphasizing forgiveness and inclusivity. Mandela's
ability to empathize with the oppressed and oppressors, his capacity for
forgiveness, and his dedication to the idea of a "rainbow nation" garnered

widespread respect and admiration. His empathetic leadership not only ended apartheid but also established a foundation for a more inclusive and just South Africa.

Empathy is a hard-earned skill, as it forces you to challenge your own biases, judgments, and ignorance. But when practiced, it creates a culture where people are encouraged to cooperate and take risks.

Adopt these three practices of empathy:

1. Consider others' perspectives: Leaders can practice empathy by putting themselves in the shoes of their team members or colleagues. This involves imagining how others might feel or think in a given situation. By considering different perspectives, you can make more informed decisions and demonstrate an understanding of the challenges and concerns your team faces.
2. Be flexible: Empathetic leaders can adapt their approach to accommodate the needs and preferences of their team members. Flexibility allows for personalized support and solutions. It shows that you respect the diverse backgrounds and working styles of your team, which can foster a more inclusive and supportive work environment.
3. Recognition and validation: Leaders can practice empathy by recognizing and validating the emotions and experiences of their teams. Acknowledging achievements, as well as the difficulties team members face, demonstrates that you value their efforts and understand their struggles. Your acknowledgment can boost morale and strengthen your leader–follower relationship.

By incorporating these empathy practices, you can create a more compassionate and supportive workplace without solely relying on active listening.

Respect Principle #3

Commitment: Commitment is crucial for leaders to establish respect in their relationships. When a leader is genuinely committed to a cause, a team, or an organization, it conveys a sense of purpose and dedication that inspires others. Your commitment demonstrates that you are not just interested in personal gain but invested in the collective success and well-being of your team or organization. Commitment means you are willing to go the extra mile, to persevere through challenges, and to lead by example. Such determination and resilience earn respect because they show that you are not only interested in the easy wins but also willing to tackle obstacles head-on and support your team in the process.

Martin Luther King Jr. was known for his unwavering commitment to a cause. The pivotal figure in the American civil rights movement in the 1950s and 1960s, King dedicated his life to advocating for racial equality and justice, particularly through nonviolent civil disobedience. His commitment to the cause of civil rights was unwavering, even in the face of considerable adversity, including threats to his personal safety. King's speeches and activities, including the 1963 March on Washington and the Montgomery bus boycott, demonstrated his profound commitment to ending racial segregation and discrimination in the United States. His dedication not only inspired millions but also earned him widespread respect, within and well beyond the civil rights movement. King's legacy continues to influence and inspire leaders and activists advocating for social justice around the world.

Commitment is fundamental to earning and maintaining respect in relationships. It signifies dedication, integrity, perseverance, and empathy, all of which contribute to a positive and respectful leadership dynamic. When people witness these qualities in you, they are more likely to reciprocate with their respect, trust, and loyalty.

Adopt these three practices of commitment:

1. Support your team consistently: Leaders can demonstrate commitment by consistently providing support and resources to their team. Your support can take the form of offering training opportunities, providing tools or materials, and being available to assist your team members when needed. Consistently being there for your team fosters respect by showing that you are committed to their success.

2. Clearly express expectations: Clearly outlining expectations and objectives for team members is another way to exhibit commitment. When you provide a structured and well-defined path forward, it communicates a commitment to helping your team achieve their

goals. Clarity is essential for establishing trust and respect within the relationship.

3. Be transparent: Leaders can build respect by being transparent about their decision-making processes and the reasoning behind their actions. Openly sharing information and the rationale for choices, even when those choices are difficult, demonstrates your commitment to honesty and fairness. Transparency can lead to respect, as it shows your dedication to maintaining trust and keeping team members informed.

Adopting these commitment practices can contribute to a strong foundation of respect for you as a leader, even without leading by example.

A final note on Chapter 11: Without establishing a firm foundation of trust and respect, you cannot build a powerful culture. And trust and respect are not something you can establish, then move on and forget about it. Leaders must be intentional like Coach K in establishing a culture where trust and respect are cultivated, encouraged, and intentionally practiced. You must consistently practice the disciplines outlined in this chapter if you want to build and maintain the trust and respect of your teams.

Chapter 11 Takeaways

- Trust and respect are the cornerstones of a successful team, be it in sports, business, or any other collaborative endeavor.
- Leaders who embrace vulnerability are better equipped to build resilient teams and inspire growth.
- A smart leader is committed to "service before self."
- Establishing values builds trust by providing a shared moral compass that guides behaviors and decisions.
- It's what you do, not what you say that builds respect.
- Consistency in attitude, effort, and communication shows your team that you embody your beliefs, values, and purpose.
- Empathy is a hard-earned skill, as it forces you to challenge your own biases, judgments, and ignorance.
- Commitment is fundamental to earning and maintaining respect in relationships.

CHAPTER 12

Communication

The Leadership Skill

As prime minister of the United Kingdom during World War II, Winston Churchill faced the daunting task of rallying the British people during a time of great peril. His speeches, delivered with an eloquence he became famous for, played a crucial role in inspiring and uniting his nation. His ability to convey a sense of resolve, courage, and determination through his words galvanized Great Britain against Nazi Germany when others in his war cabinet urged surrender. One of his most famous speeches, his "We Shall Fight on the Beaches" address delivered in 1940, is a quintessential example of his communication skills. In it, he not only acknowledged the challenges and hardships but instilled unwavering commitment in the face of extreme adversity, as so adamantly expressed in its final stanza.

"Even though large tracts of Europe and many old and famous States have fallen or may fall into the grip of the Gestapo and all the odious apparatus of Nazi rule, we shall not flag or fail."

"We shall go on to the end, we shall fight in France, we shall fight on the seas and oceans, we shall fight with growing confidence and growing strength in the air, we shall defend our Island, whatever the cost may be, we shall fight on the beaches, we shall fight on the landing grounds, we shall fight in the fields and in the streets, we shall fight in the hills; we shall never surrender, and even if, which I do not for a moment believe, this Island or a large part of it were subjugated and starving, then our Empire beyond the seas, armed and guarded by the British Fleet, would carry on the struggle, until, in God's good time, the New World, with all its power and might, steps forth to the rescue and the liberation of the old."

Churchill's leadership and communication skills helped the United Kingdom persevere during one of its darkest hours and ultimately contributed to the Allied victory in World War II. His mastery of the spoken word and his ability to connect with the public through his speeches remain a testament to the transformative power of effective communication in leadership.

Words Create Our World

One simple but profound fact every leader must embrace: *Words create our world*. For example:

- Words create light or darkness: Imagine a task that urgently needs to be completed. If a leader communicates haphazardly, it could be like trying to move quickly in darkness through an unknown room—scary, frustrating, and incredibly inefficient. However, if in the middle of the confusion, the leader explains in detail what needs to be done and how, it would be like someone turning on the lights in the unknown room, which would create clarity and accelerate movement, thought, and teamwork.

- Words create hope or despair: An ancient proverb says, "Out of the abundance of the heart, the mouth speaks." When leaders are hopeful, their communication reflects it; when leaders are in a place of despair, their communication reflects it. Words are like seeds planted in the environment, and when words are fully embedded in a culture, they produce results. Seeds of hope produce hope, and seeds of despair produce despair. Leaders must use their communication skills to perpetuate hope and drive away despair.

- Words create care or carelessness: Leaders promote care or carelessness by how they communicate intention and attention. When leaders use words to express concern, empathy, and support, they create a culture of care, which helps people feel valued and nurtured, which encourages responsible and considerate behavior, which shows up in engagement and productivity. Conversely, careless words, marked by indifference, insensitivity, or neglect, can perpetuate carelessness in actions and attitudes, which can result in a disregard for consequences or a lack of attention to the needs and feelings of others. In essence, words play a crucial role in cultivating a culture of care or carelessness in personal and cultural interactions. Care is a simple yet defining characteristic of exceptional leadership. If leaders care about people, they will be especially careful in how they communicate.

- Words create intention or indecision: Leaders can shape intention or indecision by communicating with clarity or ambiguity. When words are used with precision and purpose, they articulate clear intentions, goals, and plans, which can inspire determination and action. In contrast, vague or conflicting words can create indecision, leaving individuals uncertain about what is expected or intended. Ambiguous language breeds doubt and hesitation, making it challenging to make decisions or take action.

Leaders must be intentional, careful, and skilled in communication because language shapes perception, culture, and decision making. The way leaders communicate sets the tone for their organizations, influences employee morale, and can impact organizational policies. Effective communication builds trust, alignment, and motivation, while careless or divisive communication can lead to misunderstandings and conflict. Recognizing the power of words enables leaders to construct a positive and inclusive culture for their teams, ultimately influencing their success and the well-being of those they lead.

Defining Communication

Communication is the transfer of meaning from one person to another, from one person to many, or from groups of people to other groups. Depending on how a message is delivered determines how successful the transfer of meaning is. Often, when someone is confused or even offended by someone's communication, they respond by asking, "What do you mean by that?" If someone's communication style consistently confuses or offends, they will be labeled as rude, selfish, or careless. Conversely, if a leader is consistently clear and careful in communication, they will be perceived as thoughtful, intentional, and selfless.

The goal of every leader should be to create clarity in the PVD—purpose, vision, and discipline—of their message. Prior to communicating, a leader should ask these three questions:

1. What is the purpose of this message?
2. What is the vision I would like this message to create?
3. What communication disciplines must I maintain to fulfill the purpose and vision?

In my coaching and consulting engagements, I have seen that most leaders understand the purpose and vision of their communication, but they struggle with the disciplines. Communication is a skill with countless variables, nuances, and adjustments. I urge leaders to develop and practice their communication skills the same way a professional athlete practices the skills of their sport because if a leader is not skilled in communication, that will limit their organization's growth.

That was the case with Aaron, an owner of a commercial landscaping company. Aaron was a brilliant, hardworking, and visionary leader who could solve any landscaping challenge his clients threw at him. Because of this, his reputation grew, and his services were in high demand. But while Aaron was proficient at communicating solutions to his clients, he was not proficient at communicating his standards, expectations, and intentions to his team. As such, Aaron went from job to job instructing his crews on how he wanted things done. However, every mistake, every challenge, and every customer question became his responsibility because he was the only one with all the answers, and he became very frustrated with his supervisors' seeming lack of effort and ingenuity.

When Aaron and I first met, I was impressed by his intelligence and entrepreneurial spirit. He had an infectious energy. He explained his dilemma, that he was so frustrated that he was ready to sell his company. I explained that he wasn't alone and that his dilemma of needing to transfer his knowledge, skills, and efficacy is one that plagues many leaders. Another dilemma: His business would have little to no value without him; it would only sell if he was part of the deal.

Aaron was visibly disheartened. I encouraged him to document his thoughts, behaviors, and communication patterns by asking himself the PVD behind every solution he provided, every relationship he built, and every system he put in place. Over a few weeks, Aaron compiled pages of notes that recorded his thoughts and behaviors and sent them to me. I organized his notes and in our follow-up meeting, I posed as one of his supervisors, explaining to the best of my ability what Aaron expected of me during prospect meetings, on job sites, in handling client challenges, and in organizing crews. Aaron listened, provided some feedback, and then indicated his surprise at how well I understood his standards and expectations. I responded that if I understood this in my limited knowledge of landscaping, then his supervisors would understand it much better. Aaron and I worked on creating a training manual out of my document, and he began training his supervisors.

With the help of the manual, Aaron's communication became intentional and he began to transfer his knowledge, skills, and expectations. His supervisors practiced what he taught them, and over a three-year period, his company tripled in size. Aaron no longer had to oversee every job. He was no longer the only person with answers to problems. And his supervisors were more productive and personally fulfilled. Aaron went from being circumscribed and haphazard in his communication to intentional and transparent. He began to master communication skills that serve him to this day.

The Three Components of Communication

Dr. Albert Mehrabian, a psychologist, is known for his research on nonverbal communication, in particular, on the relative importance of different elements of nonverbal communication in conveying emotions and attitudes. His "7-38-55 Rule" suggests that communication consists of three components:

1. Words: According to Mehrabian, words themselves are responsible for only 7 percent of the emotional meaning in a message. When expressing feelings or attitudes, words alone have limited impact.
2. Tone of Voice (Paraverbals): The tone of voice, including factors like pitch, speed, and volume, accounts for 38 percent of the emotional meaning. It plays a more significant role in conveying emotions and attitudes than words.
3. Body Language: Body language, which includes facial expressions, gestures, posture, and eye contact, is responsible for the remaining 55 percent of the emotional meaning in a message. Mehrabian's research suggests these nonverbal cues have the most substantial influence on how emotions and attitudes are perceived.

Body language

Mehrabian's research indicates that while word choice is a crucial part of effective communication, the emotion behind the words, which is propelled by body language and tonality, will greatly influence the receiver's perception of the message. So how can leaders capitalize on this revelation?

Leaders' body language must convey confidence, care, and motivation. Here are six ways to improve your body language:

1. Maintain eye contact: Establishing and maintaining eye contact demonstrates confidence and sincerity.
2. Adopt an open posture: Avoid crossing arms and legs; an open posture conveys approachability and receptiveness.
3. Smile: Genuine smiles create a positive atmosphere and build rapport with others.
4. Use gestures mindfully: Employ natural and purposeful gestures to emphasize points and convey enthusiasm.
5. Control your facial expressions: Be mindful of your facial expressions to ensure they align with your intended message and project professionalism.

6. Use a firm handshake: Offer a firm and confident handshake to convey strength and assurance during your interactions.

Every leader should do body language exercises to ensure their facial expressions, hand gestures, and eye movements support the message they are delivering. Video your delivery as often as possible and use it to critique yourself. Practicing your body language will improve your connections with and reception by your audiences.

Tone

Consider the colloquialism, "It's not what you say, but how you say it that matters most." We can be right with facts, but if we're wrong in our tone, our message will fall on deaf ears. Here are six ways to improve your tone of voice in communication:

1. Modulate pitch and volume: Vary your pitch and volume to add emphasis and expressiveness, keeping your voice dynamic and engaging.
2. Speak clearly and articulately: Enunciate your words and articulate your thoughts clearly to ensure your message is easily understood.
3. Pace yourself: Avoid speaking too quickly or too slowly. Find a comfortable pace that allows for comprehension and maintains engagement.
4. Express enthusiasm: Infuse your voice with genuine enthusiasm and passion to convey a positive and motivating tone.
5. Match tone to message: Adjust your tone to align with the nature of your message. For instance, use a more empathetic tone for sensitive topics and a confident tone for decisive statements.
6. Listen to feedback: Pay attention to feedback on your communication style and be open to adjusting your tone based on the needs and preferences of your audience.

As with your body language, it's essential to record your phone calls, meetings, and other interactions to hear and assess your voice and how you can improve your tone. Improving tone will improve your connection with your audience.

Word choice

While body language and tone matter more, word choice is still vitally important to a leader's success in communication. Here are six ways to improve your word choice:

1. Be clear and concise: Use simple and straightforward language to convey your message clearly, avoiding unnecessary jargon or complex terms.
2. Adapt to your audience: Tailor your language to your audience's level of understanding, adjusting the complexity of your vocabulary to ensure comprehension. But never talk down to an audience.
3. Use positive language: Frame messages in a positive manner to inspire and motivate. Focus on solutions and opportunities rather than dwelling on problems.
4. Be empathetic: Choose words that show empathy and understanding, especially when addressing sensitive or challenging topics. Acknowledge the emotions and perspectives of others.
5. Avoid ambiguity: Be specific in your language to avoid misunderstandings. Clearly articulate your expectations and intentions to minimize confusion.
6. Inject personality: Infuse your communication with your own personality to make it authentic and relatable. People are more likely to connect with leaders who communicate in a genuine and human way.

It's important to increase your vocabulary and learn how to use the right words at the right times. *Verbal Advantage*, a graduated vocabulary-building program for professionals, is an excellent tool for improving your vocabulary and word choice.

Unifying Through Communication

President Franklin D. Roosevelt was a charismatic leader who effectively unified people through communication during one of the most challenging periods in history that included the Great Depression and World War

II. His fireside chats, a series of radio broadcasts and a hallmark of his leadership, were intimate and conversational in tone, allowing him to truly connect with U.S. citizens. During the dire economic times of the Great Depression, Roosevelt used these broadcasts to reassure and inform the public. His ability to convey empathy and understanding through the airwaves helped create a sense of national unity and trust.

As World War II unfolded, Roosevelt continued to use his communication skills to guide the nation. In his famous "Four Freedoms" speech in 1941, he articulated a vision for a world founded on essential human freedoms—freedom of speech, freedom of worship, freedom from want, freedom from fear—that not only inspired Americans but also contributed to the formation of the United Nations after the war. Roosevelt's adept use of communication in times of crisis and during periods of national transformation played a crucial role in unifying the American people and fostering resilience.

Leaders' greatest responsibility and challenge is unifying their teams. It is essential for leaders to know, understand, and employ the three intrinsic and three extrinsic motivations as they communicate with their teams.

People typically want answers to three basic questions from their leaders in relation to their work:

1. Where are we going?
2. What's required of me?
3. What's in it for me?

Where are we going? People want to know the direction the organization is taking. When they don't know where the organization is going, they experience the anxiety of uncertainty. Advertisers know the "Rule of 14," that it takes 14 impressions to make a lasting impression. Leaders can never assume they have communicated their vision so well that it has been fully comprehended and received. Regardless of how gifted a leader is, they must communicate again and again the vision of the organization and the goals of that vision. The most effective leaders also know their team members' goals and do everything in their power to help them achieve them. Do not fall into the trap of growing weary of communicating your organization's vision. Keep it fresh by trying various ways to share your vision and goals. Here are a few suggestions:

- Conduct regular team meetings to discuss the organization's vision, purpose, and goals. Use these sessions to provide updates, share progress, and address questions and concerns. This allows for real-time communication, ensuring that your team stays committed to the organization's overarching objectives. I encourage leaders to do this monthly, and if you can't do it in person, video it so those who miss it can watch it later.
- Have your marketing team develop campaigns to embed the organization's vision in team members' subconscious. Leverage internal communication platforms such as intranet sites or collaboration tools to share the organization's vision and goals. Post articles, videos, or visual presentations that articulate your strategic direction. Encourage discussions and feedback on those platforms to promote engagement and a deeper understanding of the shared vision among team members.
- Ask simple questions often. The quality of your communication is directly tied to the quality of the questions you ask. Questions are like buckets in a well, meant to draw out knowledge and understanding. Asking questions formally and informally allows leaders to determine if their vision is being grasped. If it is, they can ask follow-up questions on execution; if not, they can ask how they can improve their message.

People must know where they're going and when they've arrived. It is the leader's job to keep their team aware and engaged on the journey.

What is required of me? Remember that the greatest intrinsic motivator is to belong and contribute to a purpose bigger than self. People must know how they contribute, or they will feel their work doesn't matter and could become careless. Here are a few ways to communicate expectations and responsibilities consistently and effectively:

- Ensure that each team member has a well-defined job description outlining their responsibilities, tasks, and key performance indicators. A clear and detailed job description serves as a reference point, providing clarity on what is expected of a team member in their role. It should be a living and breathing document so that as duties and responsibilities change, the job description is updated. It should also be used to coach and mentor.

- Conduct regular one-on-one meetings with team members to discuss their roles, progress, and any adjustments to expectations. This personalized approach allows leaders to address specific concerns, provide constructive feedback, and align expectations with the individual's strengths and areas for development. This should be done at least weekly. The meetings do not have to be long, about 10 minutes generally, but they do need to be regular.

- Celebrate successes. I love the saying, "Water the flowers more than the weeds." When a team member accomplishes a task, makes an important connection, or overcomes a difficult challenge, leaders must praise them to reinforce their contribution to the organization's vision. It can be to neglect purpose and contribution. Celebrating team members' successes must never get old or stagnant. The organization that celebrates success enjoys greater success.

Leaders must be intentional in communicating what's required of each of their team members, regardless of title, tenure, or skill level.

What's in it for me (WIIFM)? Explaining "WIIFM" is crucial for leaders because it helps team members understand the personal benefits and relevance of their contributions. When your team members see the connection between their efforts and personal or professional growth, their job satisfaction tends to increase as does their motivation and commitment to the organization's goals. Clearly communicating the WIIFM factor aligns individual aspirations with organizational objectives, fostering a more engaged and productive team. Here are three ways to communicate WIIFM to your team members:

1. Emphasize how their contributions to the company's vision can lead to personal and professional growth. Highlight potential career paths, skill development opportunities, or the chance to take on challenging projects that can enhance their expertise and marketability.

2. Explain how their efforts will be recognized and rewarded, such as by acknowledgment in team meetings, performance bonuses, or other forms of recognition linked to achieving key milestones. Recognizing their contributions reinforces the value of their work and motivates sustained effort.

3. Help team members understand the broader impact of their work on the company's overall purpose. Clearly articulate how their specific roles contribute to achieving organizational goals, emphasizing the significance of their efforts in making a difference. Connecting their daily tasks to the larger purpose of the company can instill a sense of pride and personal fulfillment.

By incorporating these elements into your communication, you provide team members with a compelling answer to the WIIFM question, increasing their sense of purpose and their motivation.

By answering the questions of where are we going, what's required of me, and what's in it for me, leaders unify their teams toward a common vision, intentional focus, and short- and long-term rewards for their contributions. Again, this is not something leaders can communicate once and expect it to stick, but must do so regularly.

Handling Conflict

Where there are people, and where there is communication, there will be conflict. Nothing can strengthen a leader's resolve, confidence, and interpersonal skills more than conflict. Conflict is a positive, healthy, and unifying practice. It is often through disagreement, humility, idea sharing, and collaboration that teams strengthen ideas, relationships, and their sense of direction. Conflict should never be avoided; it should be embraced as an opportunity to improve. Unfortunately, that is not often the case. The report *Essential Conflict in the Workplace Statistics in 2023* reveals how often conflict is avoided and poorly managed.

Some statistics from the report:

- 85 percent of employees experience conflict in the workplace.
- Workplace conflict costs businesses $359 billion annually.
- 76 percent of employees prefer to avoid conflict when possible.
- 56 percent of managers report dealing with conflict in their roles.
- 60 percent of HR professionals believe that workplace conflict is due to bad management.
- Conflicts involving personality differences are the hardest to resolve (43 percent of responses).
- 95 percent of people who receive conflict resolution training say it improved their work environment.
- 41 percent of workers claim to have witnessed a conflict at work that escalated into a personal attack.
- Inclusive organizations are 120 percent more likely to resolve conflicts.
- 92 percent of employees say that resolving conflicts in a timely manner is crucial to their job satisfaction.
- 48 percent of employees believe managers need more training in handling conflicts.
- 91 percent of employees consider conflict resolution training vital to the workplace.
- After conflict resolution training, 59 percent of employees experience a decrease in workplace stress.
- One in four employees says that avoiding conflicts has led to illness or absence from work.

Unresolved conflict has deleterious results. Bitterness, resentment, hostility, anger, avoidance, gossip, blame, deflection, and poor production are just a few of the negative results of unresolved conflict. Great leaders are great conflict managers. To become proficient in conflict management, leaders must first understand the types of conflict, what happens to people when engaged in conflict, and how to resolve conflict in a calm, direct, and patient way where nobody loses.

Types of conflict: There are five major types of conflict: Information, values, interest, relationship, and structural.

1. Information conflicts arise when people have different or insufficient information or disagree over what is relevant. In these cases, leaders must guide all parties to be respectful, to be quick to listen, slow to speak, and slow to become angry. The goal is to find what the parties can agree on, and then focus on how to accommodate the areas of disagreement.

2. Values conflicts are created when people have perceived or actual incompatible belief systems. Where a person or group tries to impose its values on others or claims exclusive right to a set of values, disputes arise. It is essential that organizations create and live up to their own values and standards. If not, people will attempt to infuse their own values and standards, which could conflict with others' values and standards.

3. Interest conflicts are caused by competition over perceived or actual incompatible desires, visions, or needs. They can occur over issues of money, resources, or time. Leaders must be clear about the purpose, vision, and disciplines of their organizations. Everyone in the organization should be working for the same purpose, toward the same vision, and with the same disciplines. If not, self-interest takes over and people often mistakenly believe that in order to satisfy their own needs, those of their "opponent" must be sacrificed.

4. Relationship conflicts occur when there are misperceptions, strong negative emotions, or poor communication, so it is important to get to know your team through consistent communication, personality assessments, Q&A sessions, and goal setting. Otherwise, distrust can surface and people can begin to assume that a particular individual's actions are motivated by malice, selfishness, or an intent to harm another. The tension builds until a conflict takes place. Building relationships is an intentional practice meant to instill trust and camaraderie. To enjoy a powerful culture, leaders must facilitate relationship building, which will lead to healthy conflict.

5. Structural conflicts are caused by oppressive behaviors. Structural conflicts are prevalent in organizations where there is poor leadership, poor systems, limited resources, and limited opportunity. Typically,

those organizations need complete structural overhauls to reduce conflict. Leaders must be vigilant about their organization's leadership health, their systems, resources, and opportunities. It does not take long for a healthy, thriving organization to become unhealthy, disorganized, and full of conflict if they rest on their laurels.

What happens during conflict: When someone perceives a potential strain in a relationship, the brain responds as though facing an actual threat, initiating a physiological reaction. Positioned on either side of the brain, situated behind the optical nerves, are the amygdalae. One of their key functions is detecting fear, leading to the preparation of the body's response to the perceived threat. Consequently, in the face of a perceived threat, the amygdala activates, signaling the release of stress hormones like cortisol and adrenaline. These automatic responses, serving to save time and energy, are often instrumental in ensuring personal safety. For instance, imagine an individual standing in the middle of the road with an approaching car; it would be perilous if the brain hesitated to deliberate.

The mind and body respond in a similar way in conflict situations. This is something leaders need to understand, embrace, and learn to navigate if they are going to successfully manage conflict and teach their team to successfully manage conflicts. Too often leaders instruct their teams to ignore, avoid, suppress, or move on from conflict without addressing it. One very important statement from Sigmund Freud is, "unexpressed emotions never die." In fact, the more we try to bury a conflict, the more emotional it becomes.

Managing conflict: Regardless of the cause of conflict, great leaders shift their teams' focus from fighting to resolution. When it comes to managing conflict, there are so many variables in conflicts that it is impossible to create a single approach that will work in every situation. But we have compiled and recommend some "ground rules" for engaging conflict and its variables. A few of those ground rules:

- Privacy: There is a platitude in conflict management, "Praise in public, engage conflict in private." On the rare occasion when conflict is public, it is important that a leader immediately leads the conversation to a private place with the conflicted parties. In conflict people become defensive, and those who care about them will also become defensive when they are brought into the conflict, even if the conflict has nothing to do with them. Moving the conflict to a private place or engaging it in a private place is respectful of the parties involved—and reduces the chances it will spread.

- Focus on the problem, not the people: Remember that most conflicts in organizations are misunderstandings rooted in systems problems, unresolved conflicts that have grown, or unclear communication. However, when people are offended, their tendency is to attack the other party, assuming that they intentionally offended them or were out to get them. This is rarely true, so leaders can address the situation by saying something like, "We're here to discover the root problem. Let's focus on that, then we can discuss any offenses between us."

- Respect: You don't have to respect someone to treat them with respect. The age-old question, "Is respect given or earned?" is erroneous. The truth is, that treating people with respect in every and all situations is how people in a civilized society should behave. This is especially true in conflict. There is never a reason to treat another person with disrespect. If a party feels disrespected, they should express that without showing disrespect in return. And if the disrespect continues, they can walk away and be willing to reengage only when respect is reestablished. Conflicts where the parties are disrespectful of each other are never productive and don't get resolved.

- Validation before resolution: In conflict, it's important that each party feels validated in their frustration, offense, or interpretation. Validating someone involves empathetically acknowledging their experience. It does not mean you agree with them, only that you understand why they feel the way they do based on their perspective. When a person is validated it lowers their defenses, helps them feel connected, and allows them to see other perspectives in a nonjudgmental way. Once all parties feel validated and understood, resolution can occur.

- Resolution: Resolution is the ultimate goal of conflict management. Without a resolution, the offense cannot be put to rest. A conflict is resolved when there is:
  - Mutual agreement: All parties involved in the conflict reach a mutual agreement or consensus on the resolution. Ideally, the agreement addresses the core issues that led to the conflict.
  - Clear communication: There is clear and open communication between the parties, with a shared understanding of the resolution. Misunderstandings are clarified, and expectations are articulated.
  - Reduced tension: The emotional intensity surrounding the conflict diminishes. Tension, hostility, or negative emotions between the involved parties begin to dissipate, and there is an overall sense of relief.
  - Implementation of solutions: Agreed-upon solutions or action steps are implemented. Observable changes or progress toward resolving the initial issues should be evident.
  - Positive atmosphere: There is a shift from an atmosphere of contention to a more positive and cooperative environment. Team members or individuals involved show increased willingness to collaborate and work together.
  - Learning and growth: The conflict resolution process becomes an opportunity for learning and growth. Individuals involved gain insights into their own and others' perspectives, fostering personal and collective development.

Complete agreement on every detail of a disagreement is not always possible, but a resolution should address the fundamental issues and allow the involved parties to move forward constructively. Regular check-ins and feedback mechanisms can help ensure the resolution remains effective over time.

Letting Go: The conflict should not be discussed, repeated, or gossiped about, a condition to be agreed upon before the parties depart. Any ancillary parties who were involved or informed of the conflict should be notified that the conflict was resolved and it is no longer going to be discussed unless in a positive light. Too often, people resolve conflict, only to open it up again by discussing it with uninvolved parties after it has been resolved.

Conflict is one of the most important elements of building a powerful culture because relationships are strengthened through adversity. It is easy for people to get along when everything is going well, but you really learn about people's inner strength when you witness how they face adversity. In fact, leaders should encourage healthy conflict. Ask polarizing questions in team meetings to facilitate healthy disagreements, discussion, and resolution. Embrace conflict as a means to succeed, not a sign of failure to be avoided.

A final note on Chapter 12: Communication is a leader's greatest tool for building a powerful culture because words create our world. To be effective communicators, leaders must channel their words through intentional body language and tone. Leaders must also become masters at guiding their teams through healthy conflict in order to strengthen camaraderie, values, and bonds.

Chapter 12 Takeaways

- Leaders must be intentional, careful, and skilled in communication because language shapes perception, culture, and decision making.
- If someone's communication style consistently confuses or offends, they will be labeled as rude, selfish, or careless.
- While word choice is a crucial part of effective communication, the emotion behind the words, which is propelled by body language and tonality, will greatly influence the receiver's perception of the message.
- People must know where they're going and when they've arrived. It is the leader's job to keep their team aware and engaged on the journey.

- Leaders must be intentional in communicating what's required of each of their team members, regardless of title, tenure, or skill level.
- Nothing can strengthen a leader's resolve, confidence, and interpersonal skills more than conflict.
- Conflict is one of the most important elements of building a powerful culture because relationships are strengthened through adversity.

Additional Resources

https://mission-minded.com/when-it-comes-to-your-message-how-much-is-enough/.

www.vilendrerlaw.com/five-main-causes-conflict-mediation-can-re-solve/#:~:text=There%20are%20five%20main%20causes,relation-ship%20conflicts%2C%20and%20structural%20conflicts.

CHAPTER 13

Duplication and Succession

Creating New Leaders

In 2002, Dale and Brian Karmie left their corporate careers and moved from Northeast Ohio to Albuquerque, New Mexico, to start an artificial grass dealership as an AstroLawn franchisee. Dale and Brian expected tools, training, and mentorship from the franchisor but were pretty much left to fend for themselves those first few years, to face without support the many challenges that confront new business owners: finding reliable material suppliers, acquiring customers, complying with legal and tax regulations, recruiting and retaining team members, transportation, scheduling, developing sales and marketing strategies, financial management, delivering quality installations, and completing projects on-time and on-budget. There was a great deal of trial and error, but Dale and Brian are intentional leaders who see adversity as opportunities, and they eventually navigated their way to a successful business.

Integral to their ongoing success was assembling their team. They hired crew leaders, installers, and salespeople and even expanded their dealership into a few new markets. Their revenue was growing, their installation schedule was full, and they recognized opportunities for substantial growth. Then in 2004, they were hit with the devastating news that AstroLawn was filing bankruptcy and going out of business. That left Dale and Brian with two options: They could go back to jobs in corporate America, make a decent living, and perhaps at a later date, find another business opportunity; or they could make a bold decision and stay in the artificial turf industry and open their own business.

They chose to go bold and founded ForeverLawn in 2004. A few other AstroLawn dealers joined them and began operating under the

ForeverLawn brand, which further inspired Dale and Brian to be intentional about building ForeverLawn, which they did through purpose, vision, and discipline:

- The ForeverLawn purpose:
  Grass without Limits: a compounding statement based on the belief that people's opportunities and the impact they can have on others are limitless.
- The ForeverLawn vision:
  - To be the #1 artificial grass company in the world.
  - To be known for the highest quality products in the artificial grass industry.
  - To build a network of more than 100 ForeverLawn dealerships.
  - To help new dealers reach one million dollars in sales in their first year.
  - To set a good example for other business leaders by operating with integrity.
- ForeverLawn disciplines:
  Dale and Brian wanted to be intentional about building their business on a foundation of core values. They settled on integrity, quality, and innovation, which would inform their behavior and which they defined as:
- Integrity
  - ForeverLawn will fulfill its promises.
  - ForeverLawn will only partner with people who have integrity (dealers, vendors, and contractors).
  - ForeverLawn will only hire team members with integrity.
- Quality
  - ForeverLawn products will be built to last.
  - ForeverLawn services will be delivered with consideration, care, and excellence.
  - ForeverLawn installations will be done right, with precision and excellence.
- Innovation
  - ForeverLawn will create products to fit any application.

- ForeverLawn will always look to improve how they install their products.
- ForeverLawn will find ways to make it easier for their dealers and team members to become more successful.

Adhering to their values, and with some help from consultants, Dale and Brian built systems for sales, lead generation, and marketing. They created processes for installations, communication, and onboarding. They developed training for sales, leadership, and professional development. And they created accountability measures to ensure every dealer, from Seattle to Miami, from New York to Los Angeles, would operate similarly, achieve great results, and scale their business successfully. In everything they did, they were intentional about putting their dealers in the best position to succeed. They were unyielding in their belief that if they helped their dealers be successful, ForeverLawn would be successful.

And they were right. They went from a bootstrap startup to more than $100 million in annual sales with tens of thousands of customers, more than 70 dealers, and hundreds of team members in locations all around the world. ForeverLawn is a sponsor of the NFL Hall of Fame, NASCAR driver Jeffrey Earnhardt, and Walt Disney Parks and Resorts. They have been featured on *Today*, *DIY*, and countless television networks, including NFL Network. They have written a book, *Grass Without Limits*, documenting the beginnings of their brand. They host a podcast, "Impact Without Limits," where they encourage other business leaders to be intentional about building their businesses with integrity.

The ForeverLawn story is an excellent example of how duplication, empowerment, and accountability create scale in an organization. Dale and Brian put in the hard work of getting their thoughts, behaviors, and communication systems on paper, so that others could, and did, benefit from their example.

Duplication

"Always work yourself out of a job" was a mantra of one of my business mentors. When he first told me that, I questioned it. "If I work myself out of a job," I asked, "what will I do?" He explained that I would be forced to keep growing and moving up. True leaders never stop advancing; they never stop growing; they never stop looking for new opportunities. If a leader is too vital to their organization, it's like putting a wet blanket on a fire; it snuffs out the oxygen and the fire dies. But if a leader backs away from the fire and allows others to contribute to it, it can grow.

As well, if a leader ceases to grow, they run the risk of being smaller than those they lead. If leaders are smaller in thought, behavior, and communication than those who work for them, those people will eventually leave. Leaders must, to the best of their ability, set the standard, be the example, and then empower others to do the same.

Duplication is easy to talk about and hard to do. Especially if a leader has spent years scratching, clawing, and grinding to build a sustainable organization, allowing others to make decisions different from what they would have decided can be emotionally exhausting if a leader's ego is not in check. However, by duplicating themselves, leaders in a free-market system can build organizations that grow at scale and outlive them. The greatest leaders give up the limelight so others can shine. They let go of the steering wheel so others can drive.

One of the greatest gifts any leader can give is writing out their thoughts, behaviors, and methods of communicating. As has been repeated throughout *The Leadership Edge*, "Systems run businesses; people run systems." Leaders have their own specific systems of thought, behavior, and communication that must be passed on with intentionality for them to duplicate themselves and their impact on others successfully.

Just as with all other things in leadership, there is no one-size-fits-all to duplication, only one-size-fits-one. But there are common practices, regardless of industry, location, or position, great tools to inform your process of duplication, and, by extension, succession.

As a kid, I loved the game Simon Says. The job of the person designated as Simon was to instruct the rest of the group to do as they say. The goal was for Simon to execute the process of duplication with intentionality. Leaders must prioritize, schedule, and be accountable for the time, energy, and effort necessary to duplicate themselves. Without intentionality, duplication will not happen, succession will be haphazard, and the organization will flounder as it transitions from one leader to another.

According to a Duke University study, 91 percent of C-suite executives believe succession should be a top priority. Yet, the vast majority of organizations review their succession plan just once a year or less often. Every leader knows how important duplication is, but most fail to do it simply due to a lack of prioritization and discipline.

Common Duplication/Succession Practices

Consider the following common practices of the duplication or succession process:

- Develop a successor profile: If leaders have not identified successors, developing a successor profile is where they should begin. A successor profile ensures they do not choose a successor based solely on the relationship. Leaders often choose successors based on loyalty, longevity, and technical competencies. It is important to reward people for these traits. However, they should only play a part in choosing a successor. The right successor should have the right disposition and the people skills as well as technical competencies to handle the demands of leadership.

  Ask these questions in developing a successor profile:
  - What are the key skills and competencies required for the role?
  - How will the successor fit into the long-term goals and strategy of the organization?
  - What leadership qualities are essential for success in the position?
  - Are there certain technical or industry-specific knowledge requirements?
  - How well does the potential successor align with the company's culture and values?
  - What developmental opportunities can be provided to prepare the successor?
  - What potential challenges or obstacles might the successor may face?
  - How does the succession plan align with the organization's overall talent management strategies?
  - Are there opportunities for mentorship or coaching to support the successor's growth?

- What are the potential successor's interest in and motivation for the role?
- Have the current leader take a career and personality test: At High Performance, we use Profiles XT by Profiles International and DISC for leadership assessment.
  - Profiles XT is a comprehensive tool that assesses an individual's cognitive abilities, behavioral traits, and interests in the context of the workplace. It helps employers make more informed decisions during the hiring process and supports talent management initiatives.
  - DISC assessment is a behavioral profiling tool that helps employers understand the behavioral preferences and communication styles of their employees or potential hires. It categorizes individuals into four primary personality types: dominance (D), influence (I), steadiness (S), and conscientiousness (C).
- Create success criteria: What are the expectations and measures of success for this position? For example, consider the position of chief operating officer (COO):
  - The COO is expected to drive operational efficiency and execution across the organization, ensuring seamless day-to-day operations while aligning activities with overarching business objectives.
  - Success is measured by improvements in key operational metrics, such as cost-effectiveness, process optimization, and timely project delivery. These metrics and more will be gathered, analyzed, interpreted, and reported by the COO.
  - The COO is expected to demonstrate a keen understanding of market trends, regulatory changes, and industry best practices. And the COO must be effective in translating this knowledge into strategic initiatives to be performed by the staff.
  - Regular evaluations based on operational KPIs, feedback from department heads, and successful execution of strategic projects contribute to assessing the COO's success in optimizing and aligning operations.

- Mentor and coach the prospective new leader: Once you have
  identified a prospective duplicate or successor, it is vital to
  commit time to mentoring and then coaching that individual
  to prepare them for their new responsibilities and to help
  them get off to a good start in their new leadership role.

Thinking merely in terms of roles and responsibilities is an archaic view of a job. They are what a person has to do for the job, but what they need to do that job well is an interpretation of the job description. We recommend that you spend a year with your new leader and that you record your thoughts, ideas, and communications as you walk through your days, dictating into your phone, a notes app, a dictation machine, or hand-writing notes on your activities and interactions. Documenting your days will give your successor a real-time view of how they will engage on the job.

For example: Mike is a senior executive about to become the company's CEO and has identified an individual in the company to take over his current position. A manager comes to Mike with a problem. It's about a back order that is causing some customer friction, and he asks Mike what to do about it. Mike writes the problem down as it is expressed to him and then asks questions to get the full measure of the issue. He considers how the manager is reacting to the problem: Is he stressed out or calm and just needs some advice? If he needs to calm the manager down, that comes first, then Mike can get to the problem and make suggestions. That written record of the engagement, including the suggestions Mike makes to resolve the problem, becomes a document for sharing with his successor.

The mentoring process consists of instruction combined with a Q&A, with the protégé asking the questions. The mentor has a series of topics, all areas of responsibility—this is what you have to know and what you have to do—and uses that document to help their protégé interpret how they would approach the job. In essence, you're telling that person that their personality is different from yours, and they will address their responsibilities their own way, "but here's what I've found that works." Then the protégé opens up the Q&A, and your answers should follow the principle of being direct, simple, brief, clear, and human.

Meanwhile, coaching is founded on practices common to therapy. The coach leads the session with questions, drawing out (coaching) as opposed to dumping in (instruction). In the mentoring process, you are alongside the mentee, instructing them as they perform their roles and responsibilities. Once they become more habitual in how they are engaging those roles and responsibilities, you can become a coach. We recommend using a methodology known as the TGROW coaching model: topic, goal, reality, options, and ways forward. You start by asking them what they'd like to talk about, that is, the *topic*. Say the person answers that there's a certain individual they are having problems with. You ask, "What's your *goal*? Exactly how you will resolve this issue?" In the next phase of the process, the *reality* series of questions, you might ask, "What's working well for you at the moment?" Or "What's not working well?" In examining the *options*, you might ask, "What do you think you should do first?" Then, addressing *ways forward*, you could ask, "What will you do in the next 24 hours?"

Of course, many organizations engage professional coaches, which can be enormously productive—and profitable. One case study showed executive coaching produced a 788 percent return on investment. Additionally, the same study indicates substantially positive results from coaching:

- Improved executive productivity (reported by 53% of executives).
- Improvements in organizational strengths (48%).
- Gains in customer service (39%).
- Increased retention of executives (32%).
- Enhanced direct report/supervisor relationships (>70%).
- Improved teamwork (67%).
- Improved peer-to-peer working relationships (63%).
- Greater job satisfaction (52%).

Empower Your New Leader

Coaches are reluctant to give advice unless the coachee asks for it. That's where empowerment comes in, when a person has been given the coaching they need to ensure they are comfortable in their role and make effective decisions. Remember that our goal is to work ourselves out of a job so your duplicate or successor can take on the job. That means you're backing away and allowing the other person to be fully accountable.

In the case of succession, once you tell someone they are succeeding you, that they now have the job of CEO, you should gather the entire organization together (if possible, or at least the full executive staff), and in a ceremony, tell them their business is now in the hands of their next leader. This should be a celebration, done in a formal way, and followed up with an official written announcement.

Over the following 12 months, there should be a series of communications from the new CEO, like multiple town hall meetings, to answer questions so the team gets to know their new leader. The new leader should talk about their background and history and share their vision for the organization moving forward. A team can be riddled with fear about their futures, so the successor has to alleviate that concern by sharing their vision and ensuring everyone knows how to belong and contribute to the organization. The successor who has been empowered must now empower the organization's other leaders to find a place for everyone on the team.

A Leader Is Accountable

A leader shouldn't have to be held accountable; they should be accountable. They are accountable to everyone in the organization because leadership is about putting everyone in the best position to succeed. As opposed to telling people what to do, true leaders set their standards higher than any standards set for them, are often harder on themselves than anyone else can be, and set higher goals for themselves than others can set for them.

True leaders *are* accountable, especially to those they serve and their teams, to ensure everyone has what they need to be successful. If they do that, their teams will also hold themselves accountable.

Chapter 13 Takeaways

- True leaders never stop advancing; they never stop growing; they never stop looking for new opportunities.
- The goal is to work yourself out of a job so your duplicate or successor can take on the job.

- The greatest leaders give up the limelight so others can shine.
- Thinking merely in terms of roles and responsibilities is an archaic view of a job.
- The mentoring process consists of instruction combined with a Q&A, with the protégé asking the questions. Meanwhile, coaching is founded on practices common to therapy.
  The coach leads the session with questions, drawing out (coaching) as opposed to dumping in (instruction).
- Empower your new leaders; allow that person to be fully accountable.
- True leaders *are* accountable, especially to those they serve and their teams, to ensure everyone has what they need to be successful.

Afterword

If you've made it to this page, you've likely read the entirety of *The Leadership Edge*. It means that you've added more than 50,000 words of ideas and systems to your leadership arsenal. But nothing happens from reading; everything happens from action. That is the purpose of *The Leadership Edge*: to give you the concepts, the insights, and the tools to support your own initiative to become a more successful leader, and, by doing so, help others be successful.

My charge to you now is to take one idea, or one discipline, and act. Do not wait. Do not hesitate. Act. It is the application of education that makes a difference. And once you have mastered one discipline, promptly move to the next. Being a leader is not about fanfare, trophies, prestige, or attaining power. Leadership is an obsession to help others become their very best and ultimately to make the world a better place. That work never stops. Celebrate your successes, but don't linger. There are always more problems to solve, more people to help, more horizons to explore.

We have this one and only life, a blank canvas with a limited amount of time. Always remind yourself of your purpose, be clear about your vision, and develop the necessary disciplines to fulfill your purpose and vision. And never lose your resolve; resolve is the fire within that tells you there is something greater to achieve, something worth fighting for.

Enjoy the journey. There will be many ups and downs, triumphs and failures, the forging of strong relationships, and the breaking of weak ones. And be grateful. The challenges and adversity you will face along your journey make you stronger. They will teach you about yourself and show you what you're capable of.

As you break through, share your journey with those you lead, not to boast, but because people need hope. People need to know that the person they are following has worked through the same types of adversity they face. If you can overcome, so can they. As one of my mentors used to say, "Never trust a leader who doesn't walk with a limp."

Thank you for the honor of your time and attention. Maybe one day, our paths will cross. If they do, greet me as a friend. I wish you the best as you continue to gain *The Leadership Edge*.

Appendix

Item A: How business systems work together in a retail chain and distribution network:

- *Sales and marketing:* These intentional systems are focused on ensuring that the marketplace is aware of the organization, its offerings, and the value it provides to buyers.
- *Order placement:* The workflow begins when a customer places an order, whether through an online platform, phone call, or in-person at a physical location. The order includes specific details such as product type, quantity, and any customization or special requirements.
- *Order processing:* Once an order is received, it is processed. Here, the organization verifies product availability, checks pricing and discounts, and confirms customer information. The order is then entered into the system, and an order number or reference is assigned.
- *Inventory check and allocation:* The system checks the inventory to ensure the ordered products are available. If the items are in stock, they are allocated to the order. When an item is out of stock, the system may trigger alerts to replenish the inventory or suggest alternatives to the customer.
- *Order fulfillment:* At fulfillment, the products are prepared for delivery or pickup. This involves selecting the items from warehouse shelves, securely packaging them, and adding labels, invoices, or promotional materials as necessary.
- *Shipping and logistics:* If the order requires shipping, the organization engages a logistics and shipping provider. The system generates shipping labels, tracks the shipment, and provides the customer with relevant tracking information. For in-store pickups, the system notifies the customer when the order is ready for collection.

- *Delivery or pickup:* The customer receives the products either by delivery or visiting a designated pickup location. For deliveries, the shipping provider transports the package to the customer. In the case of in-store pickup, the customer presents the order number or identification for verification.
- *Confirmation and feedback:* Once the products are received, the customer may confirm the delivery or provide feedback on the order and their overall experience. The organization may send automated confirmation e-mails or follow-up surveys to gather feedback and ensure customer satisfaction.
- *Order completion and financials:* The workflow concludes with the completion of the order. The system updates the order status as "fulfilled" or "completed." Simultaneously, the financial system processes the payment, generates an invoice, and updates the accounts receivable or sales records.

Item B: Questions leaders can use to discover their organization's purpose and how they can employ purpose to get their team in the best position to succeed:

- Organizational identity:
  - Who are you?
- History:
  - When did your organization start?
  - Why did it start?
  - What specific problems did the founders seek to resolve?
- Strengths:
  - What do you do that is better than anyone else in your industry?
  - What are your organization's strengths? (Examples: proficient staff, hardworking, high character, brand awareness, financial strength, value proposition.)
- Passion:
  - What are you passionate about as a company?
  - What excites you?

- ○ What type of work unifies your team?
- ○ What does a great day look like for you?
- Who do you help? (from recent testimonials)
  - ○ Who was it?
  - ○ What type of business do they have?
  - ○ What did they specifically say you helped them with, the types of problems, both tangible and intangible, you resolved?
  - ○ How did the testimonial make you feel?
  - ○ What is the demographic of your best clients?
  - ○ Where are your clients?
- Why does it matter?

How does being the best of who you are, focusing on helping clients/customers, and acquiring more skills impact your business, your clients/customers, and your community?

It takes roughly nine to fourteen impressions to make a lasting impression. Therefore, communicating purpose over and again is a must for ensuring habituation in action. Ask yourself:

What does our team need to know about our purpose?
Why do they need to know it?
How can we help them remember our purpose every day?

Item C: A vision-casting Q&A exercise for leaders:

- Relative to your "broad vision" of 3, 5, 10, and 20 years:

What positive impact do you want your business to have on customers, employees, society, or the world at large?
How do you envision your business evolving over the next 3, 5, 10, and 20 years?
How will your business be unique and differentiate itself from competitors?
What do you want clients to say about your business 3, 5, 10, and 20 years from now?

How do you see your business contributing to industry innovation or pushing boundaries?

What will your annual revenue be 3, 5, 10, and 20 years from now?

What role does sustainability or social responsibility play in your business's vision?

How will your business leverage or innovate emerging technologies or trends to stay relevant and competitive?

How do you see your business adapting to changing customer needs and preferences?

What kind of culture do you want to foster within your organization, and how will it contribute to your vision?

How will your business empower and develop your employees to drive growth and success? Be specific.

How do you envision your business's relationship with its stakeholders, such as customers, suppliers, and the local community?

What will be the measure of success for your business beyond financial performance?

After you have answered the questions and written down your answers, ask yourself: "How will we know if we have achieved our vision in each of these areas?" If you can't measure achievement or progress, your answers are not specific enough and should be revisited and amended. When they are measurable, they can become narrow and actionable.

• Relative to your "narrow vision" of one year:

What specific accomplishments and milestones do you want your business to achieve within the next year?

What new products, services, or features do you plan to introduce in the next year?

How do you envision your customer base growing or evolving over the next year?

What steps will you take to improve customer satisfaction and loyalty in the next year?

How will you enhance your marketing and branding efforts to increase awareness and reach?

What key partnerships or collaborations do you plan to establish in the next year?

How will you leverage technology or digital advancements to streamline operations or improve efficiency?

What initiatives will you undertake to strengthen your business's financial position in the next year?

How will you invest in the development and growth of your employees in the next year?

What steps will you take to enhance your business's competitiveness within the market?

How will you measure and track progress toward your goals throughout the year?

What specific strategies will you implement to expand your customer base or target new markets?

How will you improve your business's online presence and engage with customers through digital channels?

What steps will you take to enhance your business's sustainability and best practices?

How will you proactively reach out for customer feedback and incorporate it into your business decisions and improvements?

When you have answers that are specific and measurable, write them down. Your next step is to disseminate your vision based on categories or departments:

- Sales and Marketing
- Operations
- Finance and Administration
- Culture and Human Resources
- Executive Leadership

This step is vital because without it, your organizational vision will be too broad. You won't connect with key stakeholders, and most likely, you won't be able to convert your vision into actionable disciplines.

Item D: Develop your own list from these answers to "What are your natural strengths?"

- Leadership skills: The ability to inspire and guide others toward a common goal.
- Creativity: Thinking outside the box and generating innovative ideas and solutions.
- Empathy: Understanding and connecting with others' emotions and experiences.
- Communication: Articulating ideas clearly and effectively to others.
- Problem-solving: Analyzing issues and finding effective ways to address them.
- Resilience: Bouncing back from setbacks and maintaining a positive outlook.
- Adaptability: Being flexible and open to change in various situations.
- Perseverance: Sustained effort and determination to achieve goals.
- Curiosity: A desire to explore and learn about new topics and concepts.
- Analytical thinking: Examining information critically and making well-informed decisions.
- Intuition: Trusting gut feelings and instincts in decision making.
- Collaboration: Working effectively with others in a team-oriented environment.
- Organization: Keeping tasks and responsibilities well-structured and manageable.
- Emotional intelligence: Being aware of and managing one's emotions and understanding others' emotions.
- Time management: Efficiently allocating time to tasks and prioritizing responsibilities.
- Attention to detail: Noticing and addressing small elements that can impact the bigger picture.
- Patience: Remaining composed and understanding in challenging situations.
- Public speaking: Delivering engaging and impactful speeches or presentations.

- Humor: Bringing joy and laughter to others through wit and humor.
- Empowerment: Helping others realize and leverage their own strengths and potential.

Item E: Examples to help you answer, "What skills have you learned or mastered through education, practice, and experience?"

- Technical skills: Proficiency in using specific tools, software, or equipment related to a particular field or profession.
- Critical thinking: The ability to analyze, evaluate, and synthesize information to make informed decisions.
- Research skills: Gathering and evaluating data, conducting studies, and drawing conclusions from reliable sources.
- Writing skills: Communicating effectively through written content, including reports, essays, and professional communication.
- Presentation skills: Delivering information and ideas in a clear, engaging, and persuasive manner to an audience.
- Problem-solving: Applying logical thinking and creativity to address challenges and find solutions.
- Data analysis: Interpreting and drawing insights from datasets using various analytical techniques and tools.
- Project management: Planning, organizing, and executing projects within specific timelines and budgets.
- Negotiation skills: Reaching agreements and resolving conflicts through effective communication and compromise.
- Leadership and management: Guiding and motivating teams to achieve shared objectives and oversee organizational processes.
- Adaptability: Adjusting to changing circumstances and learning to thrive in new environments.
- Teamwork and collaboration: Working harmoniously with others to achieve common goals and foster a productive work environment.

- Financial literacy: Understanding financial concepts, budgeting, and managing personal or organizational finances.
- Networking: Building and maintaining professional relationships to expand opportunities and connections.
- Foreign languages: Proficiency in speaking, writing, and understanding languages other than one's native tongue.
- Time management: Efficiently allocating time and prioritizing tasks to increase productivity.
- Customer service: Providing excellent service and support to meet the needs of clients or customers.
- Conflict resolution: Handling disputes and finding resolutions to maintain positive relationships.
- Public speaking: Effectively delivering speeches or presentations to inform or persuade an audience.
- Sales and marketing: Promoting products or services and persuading potential customers to make purchases.

Item F: Questions that serve as a guide for you to develop your own personal vision:

- Relationships and family:
  - What kind of relationships do I want to cultivate with my family and loved ones?
  - How can I prioritize my time and meaningful connections with the people I care about?
  - What values and principles do I want to instill in my relationships and family dynamics?
  - How can I contribute to the growth and well-being of my family members?
  - What does a fulfilling and harmonious family life look like to me?
- Career:
  - What kind of work or profession aligns with my passions and interests?
  - What skills and strengths do I want to leverage in my career?

- What impact do I want to make through my work?
- What opportunities and challenges do I want to pursue for professional growth?
- How can I strike a balance between personal fulfillment and financial stability in my career?
- Health:
  - What does optimal physical and mental health mean to me?
  - How can I incorporate regular exercise and healthy eating habits into my lifestyle?
  - What self-care practices can I adopt to maintain my overall well-being?
  - What steps can I take to manage stress and cultivate a positive mindset?
  - What health goals do I want to achieve and sustain for the long term?
- Finances:
  - What are my financial goals and aspirations?
  - How can I develop effective budgeting and saving habits?
  - What strategies can I implement to manage debt and achieve financial stability?
  - How can I create multiple streams of income and build wealth over time?
  - What does financial freedom mean to me and how can I work toward it?
- Hobbies and interests:
  - What activities or hobbies bring me joy and fulfillment?
  - How can I prioritize time for my hobbies amidst other responsibilities?
  - What new interests or skills do I want to explore and develop?
  - How can I incorporate creativity and leisure into my daily life?
  - What goals or milestones do I want to achieve in my hobbies or personal interests?

- Self-education:
  - What subjects or areas of knowledge do I want to learn more about?
  - How can I incorporate continuous learning and personal growth into my routine?
  - What resources or learning methods can I use to expand my knowledge?
  - What skills or certifications do I want to acquire for personal or professional development?
  - How can I challenge myself intellectually and embrace a lifelong learning mindset?
- Personal skills:
  - What skills or abilities do I want to develop and excel in?
  - How can I identify and leverage my existing strengths?
  - What steps can I take to improve my communication and interpersonal skills?
  - How can I enhance my problem-solving and decision-making capabilities?
  - What opportunities or experiences can I seek to enhance my personal skills and broaden my perspective?
- Charity:
  - What causes or social issues resonate with me and align with my values?
  - How can I contribute my time, resources, or skills to make a positive impact?
  - What charities or organizations do I want to support and be involved in?
  - How can I cultivate a spirit of empathy and compassion toward others?
  - What legacy of giving back do I want to create and leave behind?

Chapter 4 Appendix

Systems evaluation: Questions to ask employees to assess the effectiveness and efficiency of their organization's systems:

Process clarity

- Do you have a clear understanding of the processes and procedures related to your job?
- Are the documented processes up to date and easily accessible?
- Are there any bottlenecks or areas where the process flow could be improved?
- Are there steps in the process that seem unnecessary or redundant?

System integration:

- Are the technological systems and software used in our organization effectively integrated?
- Do you encounter any difficulties or inefficiencies when transferring data between different systems?
- Are there any opportunities for automation or streamlining tasks through system integration?
- Are critical functionalities missing in our current systems?

Data management

- How well is data captured, stored, and managed within our systems?
- Are the data entry processes accurate and reliable?
- Are there any challenges or limitations in accessing and analyzing data?
- Are we effectively utilizing data to make informed business decisions?

Communication and collaboration

- How well do our systems facilitate communication and collaboration among team members?
- Are there any challenges or gaps in sharing information or documents?
- Do you feel that the systems adequately support teamwork and efficient collaboration?
- What are your suggestions for improving communication and collaboration through system enhancements?

User experience

- How user-friendly are the tools you use on a daily basis?
- Are there any features or functionalities that are difficult to navigate or understand?
- Do you receive sufficient training and support to use the systems effectively?
- What are your recommendations for improving the user experience and making the systems more intuitive?

Reliability and performance

- How reliable and stable is your technology in terms of uptime and performance?
- Do you experience frequent system crashes, slow response times, or other technical issues?
- Are there any specific areas where the system performance could be enhanced?
- Are there any security concerns or vulnerabilities that need to be addressed?

Continuous improvement

- What are your suggestions for enhancing the existing systems or implementing new technologies?

- What industry best practices or emerging trends should we consider incorporating into our systems?
- How can we encourage employee feedback and involvement in improving our systems?
- What training or resources are needed to support ongoing system improvements?

Roles and responsibilities: Questions for leaders to ask their direct reports to assess their understanding of their roles and responsibilities:

Role clarity

- Can you describe your primary responsibilities and tasks within your role?
- How well do you understand the expectations and objectives of your position?
- Are there any aspects of your role that you find unclear or confusing?
- Do you feel that your role aligns with the goals and vision of the organization?

Goal alignment

- How well do you understand how your individual goals contribute to the overall team or department objectives?
- Are there any areas where you require more clarity on how your work ties into the broader organizational goals?
- Do you have the necessary resources and support to achieve your goals effectively?
- Are there any obstacles or challenges preventing you from fulfilling your responsibilities?

Performance measurement

- Are you aware of the key performance indicators (KPIs) that are used to evaluate your performance?

- How often do you receive feedback on your performance and progress?
- Do you have a clear understanding of the criteria used to assess your success in your role?
- Are there any specific areas where you believe your performance could be improved?

Collaboration and communication

- Are you clear on your role in cross-functional or interdepartmental collaborations?
- Do you understand how your work impacts and interacts with the work of others in the organization?
- Are there any challenges or gaps in communication between you and your colleagues or superiors?
- Are you aware of the channels and tools available for effective communication within the organization?

Development and growth

- Do you feel that you have opportunities for professional development and growth?
- Are there any skills or areas of knowledge you would like to develop further?
- Are you receiving sufficient support and feedback from your supervisor to help you grow in your role?
- Are there any suggestions or recommendations you have for enhancing your development within the organization?

Support and resources

- Do you have the necessary resources, tools, and equipment to perform your job effectively?
- Are there any training needs or additional support you require to excel in your responsibilities?

- Are there any obstacles or constraints that hinder your productivity or ability to meet expectations?
- Do you feel that you have the appropriate level of autonomy and authority to carry out your responsibilities?

Expectations and feedback

- Are you clear on the performance expectations for your role?
- How often would you like to receive feedback on your performance and progress?
- Do you feel comfortable approaching your supervisor with questions or concerns regarding your responsibilities?
- Are there any areas where you believe you need more guidance or feedback to excel in your role?

Notes

Chapter 1

1. Gurdjian, Halbeisen, and Lane (2014).
2. Kellerman (2012).
3. Wellable (2023).
4. Nink and Jennifer (2023).
5. Ibid.
6. Built In (2024).
7. Inc.Com (2024).
8. POWERS (2022).
9. Inc.Com (2024).

Chapter 2

1. Rost (1993).
2. Stutz (2022).

Chapter 3

1. Barry (1982).

Chapter 4

1. Vaughan et al. (1979).
2. Karmie and Karmie (2015).

Chapter 5

1. Belic, Shimizu, Reid, Hillgrove, Adler, and Shimoff (2012).
2. Picchi (2023).
3. Michael Lee Stallard (2008).
4. Berkman (2018).

5. Earls (2024).
6. Tracy (2024).
7. Wanderlust Worker (2024).

Chapter 6

1. Huberman (2021).
2. Rohn (2024).
3. Lewis (2024).

Chapter 7

1. Baldwin (2024).
2. MindTools (2024).

Chapter 8

1. Tracy (2022).
2. Dispenza (2018).

Chapter 10

1. Schein and Schein (2017).

Chapter 12

1. UTPB (2023).
2. Elster (2000).
3. Pollack Peacebuilding Systems (2023).
4. Freud (2024).

Chapter 13

1. Korn Ferry (2023).
2. Anderson (1970).

References

Chapter 1

1. Gurdjian, P., T. Halbeisen, and K. Lane. January 1, 2014. *Why Leadership-Development Programs Fail.* McKinsey & Company. www.mckinsey.com/featured-insights/leadership/why-leadership-development-programs-fail.
2. Kellerman, B. 2012. *The End of Leadership.* Harper Business.
3. "9 Employee Engagement Statistics You Should Know for 2023." October 31, 2023. Wellable. www.wellable.co/blog/employee-engagement-statistics-you-should-know/#:~:text=85%25%20of%20employees%20are%20not%20engaged%20at%20work,-According%20to%20Gallup's&text=Specifically%2C%2085%25%20of%20employees%20are,bare%20minimum%20required%20of%20t.
4. Nink, M. and J. Robison. October 9, 2023. "How to Ensure Employees Speak up About Ethical Issues." Gallup.Com: Gallup. www.gallup.com/workplace/319619/ensure-employees-speak-ethical-concerns.aspx.
5. Ibid.
6. "38 Employee Turnover Statistics to Know." n.d. Built In. builtin.com/recruiting/employee-turnover-statistics (accessed January 8, 2024).
7. "Survey: 91 Percent of 1,000 Employees Say Their Bosses Lack." n.d. Inc.Com. www.inc.com/marcel-schwantes/survey-91-percent-of-1000-employees-say-their-boss.html (accessed January 8, 2024).
8. "Promote Frontline Leaders From Within Your Organization." August 10, 2022. POWERS. www.thepowerscompany.com/resources/front-line-leaders-promotion/.
9. *"Survey: 91 Percent of 1,000 Employees Say Their Bosses Lack ..."* n.d. Inc.Com, www.inc.com/marcel-schwantes/survey-91-percent-of-1000-employees-say-their-boss.html (accessed 8 January, 2024).

Chapter 2

1. Rost, J.C. 1993. *Leadership for the Twenty-First Century*. Praeger.
2. *Stutz*. 2022. Directed by Jona Hill, Produced by Jona Hill. Netflix app.

Chapter 3

1. Barry, P. 1982. "The Tradition of Spontaneous Order." In *Literature of Liberty*. 5 vols. https://en.wikipedia.org/wiki/Norman_P._Barry.

Chapter 4

1. Vaughan, B. et al. 1979. *The Best of Bill Vaughan*. Independence Press.
2. Karmie, D. and B. Karmie. 2015. *Grass Without Limits: Personal Freedom, Family, Faith, and ForeverLawn*. Self-Published.

Chapter 5

1. Belic, R., E.H. Shimizu, F. Reid, V. Hillgrove, M. Adler, and M. Shimoff. 2012. *Happy*. [Place of publication not identified], Wadi Rum Films.
2. Picchi, A. March 10, 2023. "One Study Said Happiness Peaked at $75,000 in Income. Now, Economists Say It's Higher—by a Lot." CBS News, CBS Interactive. www.cbsnews.com/news/money-happiness-study-daniel-kahneman-500000-versus-75000/.
3. "Today's Lack of Human Connection Affects Happiness and Employee Engagement." October 1, 2008. Michael Lee Stallard. www.michaelleestallard.com/todays-lack-of-human-connection-affects-happiness-and-employee-engagement.
4. Berkman, E.T. March 1, 2018. "The Neuroscience of Goals and Behavior Change." *Consulting Psychology Journal*. U.S. National Library of Medicine. www.ncbi.nlm.nih.gov/pmc/articles/PMC5854216/.

5. Earls, A. 2024. "Americans' Views of Life's Meaning and Purpose Are Changing." Lifeway Research. research.lifeway.com/2021/04/06/americans-views-of-lifes-meaning-and-purpose-are-changing/.

6. Tracy, B. n.d. Brian Tracy Quote. tracy2256.rssing.com/chan-45232282/index-latest.php (accessed January 18, 2024).

7. "The Harvard MBA Business School Study on Goal Setting." n.d. Wanderlust Worker. www.wanderlustworker.com/the-harvard-mba-business-school-study-on-goal-setting/ (accessed January 18, 2024).

Chapter 6

1. Huberman, A. 2021. "Controlling Your Dopamine for Motivation, Focus & Satisfaction | Huberman Lab Podcast #39." YouTube, televised on September 27, 2021. www.youtube.com/watch?v=QmOF-0crdyRU.

2. Rohn, J. n.d. "AZ Quotes: Jim Rohn." www.azquotes.com/quote/814910 (accessed January 18, 2024).

3. Lewis, C.S. n.d. "A Quote by C.S. Lewis." Goodreads. www.goodreads.com/quotes/52604-education-without-values-as-useful-as-it-is-seems-rather (accessed January 18, 2024).

Chapter 7

1. Baldwin, C. n.d. "A Quote by Christina Baldwin." Goodreads. www.goodreads.com/quotes/103158-journal-writing-is-a-voyage-to-the-interior (accessed January 18, 2024).

2. "The Johari Window." n.d. MindTools. www.mindtools.com/au7v71d/the-johari-window (accessed January 18, 2024).

Chapter 8

1. Tracy, B. April 30, 2022. *Goals by Brian Tracy*. YouTube. www.youtube.com/watch?v=usd5IHvaGW0.

2. Dispenza, J. 2018. *Breaking the Habit of Being Yourself: How to Lose Your Mind and Create a New One*. Hay House.

Chapter 10

1. Schein, E.H. and P. Schein. 2017. *Organizational Culture and Leadership*. Wiley.

Chapter 12

1. "How Much of Communication Is Nonverbal?: UT Permian Basin Online." May 15, 2023. UTPB. online.utpb.edu/about-us/articles/communication/how-much-of-communication-is-nonverbal/.
2. Elster, C.H. 2000. *Verbal Advantage: 10 Easy Steps to a Powerful Vocabulary*. Random House
3. "Workplace Conflict Statistics 2023: Pollack Peacebuilding." December 1, 2023. Pollack Peacebuilding Systems. pollackpeacebuilding.com/workplace-conflict-statistics/.
4. Freud, S. n.d. "Sigmund Freud Quote." AZ Quotes. www.azquotes.com/quote/453097 (accessed January 19, 2024).

Chapter 13

1. "Revamping Succession Planning." November 17, 2023. Korn Ferry. www.kornferry.com/institute/revamping-succession-planning.
2. Anderson, M.C. 1970. "Executive Briefing: Case Study on the Return on Investment of Executive Coaching." MetrixGlobal. researchportal.coachingfederation.org/Document/Pdf/abstract_681.

About the Authors

High Performance Principal **Michael B. Ross** has worked with hundreds of business owners and executives, from large corporations to small businesses, helping them become more effective leaders who inspire their employees and grow their revenues. As a college athlete and during his service with the U.S. Navy, Michael learned that intentional actions combined with strategic disciplines can create exceptional outcomes. He witnessed firsthand the power of unified teams and quality leadership. In building his firm and programs, he has used his education and experience to help leaders clarify their vision and enact real behavioral change in their organizations. Michael received his master's in Organizational Leadership from Geneva College and his master's in Project Management from Robert Morris University. He has earned coaching and consulting certifications from Team.

Mike Shaw is the author of *The Musician*, a work of literary fiction published by Blue Room Books in June 2021, and coauthor of *Understanding Economic Equilibrium* with Federal Reserve Chief Economist Thomas J. Cunningham, PhD, published by Business Expert Press also in June 2021. He has followed a double career path as a musician and writer. A singer-pianist, he began touring in the late 1960s, performing in nightclubs and on concert stages, solo, and with jazz combos, ultimately settling in New Orleans in the late 70s. As a writer, he counts more than 15,000 published articles, from investigative pieces adapted by *60 Minutes* and *ABC 20/20* to ghostwritten articles, white papers, and blogs for corporate clients. He has founded and presided over three Atlanta-based marketing agencies, including currently, Shade Communications. He is a jazz columnist for *The Atlanta Journal-Constitution* and Atlanta's arts community online publication, *ArtsATL*, and cohosts a weekly podcast, *Music Life and Times*, with internationally renowned jazz pianist Kevin Bales. He holds an MA in English from the University of Miami.

Index

OTHER TITLES IN THE HUMAN RESOURCE MANAGEMENT AND ORGANIZATIONAL BEHAVIOR COLLECTION

Michael J. Provitera and Michael Edmondson, Editors

- *Ignite All* by The Fusion Team
- *(Re)Value* by Adam Wallace and Adam Wallace
- *Dysfunctional Organizations* by David D. Van Fleet
- *The Negotiation Edge* by Michael Saksa
- *Applied Leadership* by Sam Altawil
- *Forging Dynasty Businesses* by Chuck Violand
- *How the Harvard Business School Changed the Way We View Organizations* by Jay W. Lorsch
- *Managing Millennials* by Jacqueline Cripps
- *Personal Effectiveness* by Lucia Strazzeri
- *Catalyzing Transformation* by Sandra Waddock
- *Critical Leadership and Management Tools for Contemporary Organizations* by Tony Miller
- *Leading From the Top* by Dennis M. Powell
- *Warp Speed Habits* by Marco Neves
- *I Don't Understand* by Buki Mosaku
- *Nurturing Equanimity* by Michael Edmondson

Concise and Applied Business Books

The Collection listed above is one of 30 business subject collections that Business Expert Press has grown to make BEP a premiere publisher of print and digital books. Our concise and applied books are for...

- Professionals and Practitioners
- Faculty who adopt our books for courses
- Librarians who know that BEP's Digital Libraries are a unique way to offer students ebooks to download, not restricted with any digital rights management
- Executive Training Course Leaders
- Business Seminar Organizers

Business Expert Press books are for anyone who needs to dig deeper on business ideas, goals, and solutions to everyday problems. Whether one print book, one ebook, or buying a digital library of 110 ebooks, we remain the affordable and smart way to be business smart. For more information, please visit www.businessexpertpress.com, or contact sales@businessexpertpress.com.

www.ingramcontent.com/pod-product-compliance
Lightning Source LLC
Chambersburg PA
CBHW061210220326
41599CB00025B/4592